Boundless

HENRY KING | VALA AFSHAR

Boundless

A NEW MINDSET
FOR UNLIMITED
BUSINESS SUCCESS

WILEY

For general information on our other products and services or for technical support, please contact our Customer Care Department within the United States at (800) 762-2974, outside the United States at (317) 572-3993 or fax (317) 572-4002.

Wiley also publishes its books in a variety of electronic formats. Some content that appears in print may not be available in electronic formats. For more information about Wiley products, visit our web site at www.wiley.com.

Library of Congress Cataloging-in-Publication Data is Available:

ISBN 9781394171798 (Cloth)
ISBN 9781394171804 (ePub)
ISBN 9781394171811 (ePDF)

Cover Design: Wiley

SKY10051758_072423

This book is dedicated to our families, with our undying love and gratitude.

(Henry) To my parents, Ian and Shirley, who gave me the best start in life. To my boys, Alex and Will, of whom I could not be more proud. And above all to my wife, Sarah, who is more important to me than I can say. I love you all and hope that I have made you proud in return.

(Vala) To my heroes, my mom and dad, Showkat Rafi and James Afshar, who shaped who I am. To my beautiful wife and best friend, Stacey, who is my first love and the very best partner in life. And to my purpose and greatest achievements in life, my three amazing children: Donya, Pari, and Vala. I love you all.

Contents

Preface
The Journey to Boundless

Our companies and institutions today are not organized to deliver *customer* success; they're organized to accumulate and protect their resources and to extract maximum value from them for their *own* success. It's an old business model that is grounded in the ideas of structure and control, independence and strength. In times of relative stability it worked very well. However, in this age of accelerating technological innovation, of increasingly empowered individuals, and of ongoing societal crises, we need a new model.

We created that model, and we've titled it Boundless. It's a model organized for the success of not only the company itself but also of its customers and employees—as well as of all other partners and rights owners, including community and environment. It is a model that lives in flow, in connectedness, and in responsiveness. It is a model that is optimistic; it sees opportunities where others may only see danger, and it sees value in gratitude and reciprocity. Boundless is the redefinition of resource management, the operating model for the future of success.

Our Journey to Boundless

The two of us were on quite different paths when we first recognized Boundless as an emerging and important phenomenon—but we met at a critical juncture in 2017 and have since continued the journey together. We'll next share our individual paths.

Henry's Path

For me it started a long time ago, in 1995, when a friend recommended I read Kevin Kelly's *Out of Control: The New Biology of Machines, Social Systems, and the Economic World*. I had already begun to turn my attention to the complicated relationship between nature and technology, but this book exposed me to new ideas and in some ways changed my life. I became impatient for Kelly's next book, and was intrigued to learn that he was asking himself a non-obvious question, namely, "what does technology want?" While I waited, I decided to contemplate the question myself.

I started with something that was already close to me: the origin of storytelling. Homer's *Iliad* and *Odyssey* were core texts for me as a former student of classical literature, and one of the perennial questions regarding these epic poems is the nature of their origin. Did they start as oral stories that were later written down, or were they written down from the start? Another consideration is the difference between the two models in story creation: performance and repetition. In the oral tradition, stories are recited from memory and are adapted, or not, as appropriate for the occasion and the audience. Repetition and dispersion of the story are a slow process—in which multiple tellings from multiple storytellers produce multiple variations.

By contrast, the written tradition requires no memorization because the story has been recorded—or captured—using at a minimum the products of two technologies: a marking device and a markable surface. This act of capture separates out the acts of creation, memorization, and performance from one another and in doing so enables at least four remarkable things: accurate retelling of the story, accurate reproduction of the story (even in multiple copies), greater speed, and range of reproduction and/or transmission.

In 2009, the year before Kelly's book *What Technology Wants* finally became available, Brian Arthur published *The Nature of Technology*. In that book, Arthur's definition of technology as "phenomena captured and put to use" gave me the confidence that I was on the right track. The word *captured*, however, now felt like a confluence or conflation of three ideas that could be usefully teased apart. The first is the idea of stopping or arresting. It's difficult to capture something while it's in motion, and so stopping it becomes central to the process. The second is the idea of decoupling. Capturing something or someone requires that they are taken out of their environment or context or community. The third is the idea of containing or storing or imprisoning. Arresting/stopping, decoupling/extracting, containing/storing: three powerful and related but distinct acts—given perhaps too little attention within the single word *capture*.

I soon realized that it's not just phenomena that we capture and put to use. We apply the same logic to just about anything we think can be useful to us. We have turned the world into a world of resources. All of our industries are involved in capturing resources and putting them to use.

And yet there are exceptions: experiences and products and business models that seem to be more concerned with freeing up resources, sharing them, enabling and supporting their flow, instead of capturing them. In their article "Abandon Stocks, Embrace Flows" in the January 2009 edition of *Harvard Business Review*, John Hagel III, John Seely Brown, and Lang Davison highlighted this distinction in regard to knowledge resources, urging their readers to abandon stocks of knowledge and instead embrace their flow. I realized this could apply just as equally to other resources, and set out to explore what that might mean.

Fast-forward nearly a decade; by the time I met Vala in 2017, I was convinced that flow was not only applicable to all resources and all industries, but that it could be a compelling and even preferable alternative to the dominant capture or silo model.

Vala's Path

My family and I immigrated from Iran to the United States as refugees. As my parents struggled to rebuild their lives they worked two jobs, seven days a week, for nearly 25 years. I lived a happy life, with two loving parents and a younger sister, but it was a hard life. I adopted a silo mindset—capture resources, protect them, and extract their value—that led to a strong commitment to education and even a stronger commitment to the work ethics I learned from my parents. After spending seven years pursuing undergraduate and graduate studies in electrical engineering, while working more than full-time during the entire journey, I began my career as a software engineer in the technology sector.

My work ethic and ability to establish trust among peers and business leaders led to my being given the opportunity to lead projects and people. After just my first year on the job I was promoted to engineering project leader, and subsequently to vice president of engineering, chief customer officer responsible for global service operations, and chief marketing officer of a public enterprise company with $650 million in annual revenues. I believe that my career was fast tracked when I strayed from my silo mentality and began adopting a mindset based on optimizing flow of value and shared success.

My mindset and leadership philosophy was strongly influenced by Marc Benioff, founder of Salesforce—particularly the importance of collaboration and the social enterprise. It was 2009, at Salesforce's annual conference. Benioff's keynote focused on the importance of social collaboration, minimizing business friction, and creating a culture where it's not the best titles that win, but the best ideas. In a social business, the ideas are heard and seen throughout the fabric of the organization, not just at the top of the organizational chart. In 2011, I filed for a US patent for technology that would invite machines to the business social graph. This patent includes the ability to communicate with internet-connected devices using public social networks and public cloud computing infrastructure. I'm proud to say I was awarded the patent in 2018: for a machine-to-machine and human-to-machine communication platform using public and private social networks—Facebook, Twitter, and Salesforce Chatter.

In 2012, I coauthored a book titled *The Pursuit of Social Business Excellence*, which referenced my invention and the importance of using customer relationship management (CRM) solutions to improve the connections, mobility, and speed of value creation for all stakeholders—employees, customers, and business partners. I emphasized the importance of deliberately removing friction in business, in part by employing the success factors of culture, people, process, and technology. The book also outlined the core competencies of being a customer company, highlighting core values, culture, and servant leadership as key drivers of sustained momentum and growth in business. This book led to a practice of writing weekly articles for major US publications and producing a live weekly video show *DisrupTV* (launched in 2013) on disruptive innovation, leadership, and business practices. I have written over 750 articles in the last decade and interviewed more than 1,300 executives, authors, and entrepreneurs on my weekly show—which has been watched by more than 2 million viewers.

The most disruptive change in my behavior was using social media, specifically Twitter, starting in 2011. When I recognized the power of social collaboration on Twitter my silo-based mindset began shifting to a flow-based mindset. Today, I have over 1 million followers on Twitter, and I produce billions of impressions every year. In 2015, after a 12-year journey of being a Salesforce trailblazer customer, I was invited to join Salesforce as their chief digital evangelist.

In summary, Boundless opportunities have been offered to me on account of my shifting my mindset from one of silos to one of flows. When I met Henry in 2017, we immediately recognized the many ways our mindsets overlap, and began working on a framework that captures our approach to problem-solving and value creation. The result of five years of collaboration and lessons learned have led to this book: a guide to accelerating growth and impact using seven principles that can significantly enhance individual, team, and company outcomes.

Our Continued Journey Together

The two of us first met in 2017 as part of a Salesforce team working with a customer in the higher education space to explore models for lifelong learning focused on student-owned journeys and data, multiple and verifiable credentials, and nontraditional and multi-provider pathways. We discussed this as a fundamentally flow-based model and thereafter began to work together to investigate its relevance across multiple industries and regions. We began to pay more attention to the ongoing and accelerating evolution of our digital technologies and the new opportunities they bring to those able to perceive and assimilate them, as well as of course the new challenges they bring to those who aren't. The gulf between opportunity and challenge, between success and failure, was made manifest by the COVID-19 pandemic, which quickly became *the* accelerant of digital adoption, at least for the connections between businesses and their customers and employees in a digital-first, work-from-anywhere—in fact, do anything from anywhere—world.

We were originally using the word *flow* as an umbrella term for this new model, but as we have continued our exploration we have become increasingly aware of the changing "shape" of companies, of what they need to look like in the new world of business ecosystems, remote and autonomous workforces, and globally connected customers. And as we have looked for ways to describe the company of the future, at least from an organizational and resource management perspective, we have come to the realization that *flow* doesn't quite work in the way that we want it to. *Flow* is important because it emphasizes the need for companies to put their resources in motion rather than accumulating and controlling them, but it misses two of the most important features of digital technologies, namely, the ability of everything to be connected to everything else and the ability of everything to have intelligence and self-determination, otherwise known as *autonomy*. And, finally, *flow* misses the other key feature of the connected world: the economy of abundance—especially the abundance of ideas, of innovation and creativity, and of the energy it generates.

As we've already said, we consider this new model for business success the Boundless company: the logical evolution of the *connected* company for the digital-first, decentralized-everything world. In this new world, successful companies need to be Boundless in several ways.

To be successful, companies need to be Boundless in their energy and their enthusiasm for the success of their customers, employees, partners, and communities.

To be successful, companies need to be Boundless in their ability to transcend the physical limits of their office spaces and become effective orchestrators of their remote, distributed workforce and other resources. As we have already discussed, the office has traditionally provided a clear sense of belonging, a demarcation line between those who are part of the company and those who are not. And it also provided a clear sense of hierarchy, between those who inhabit cubicles and those with private offices, between those on lower floors and those on high. Nowadays, with a remote workforce, companies need new ways to engender belonging based more on purpose and values-based inclusion than on location-based exclusion—as well as new ways to drive toward desired outcomes more by mission-based orchestration than by control-based supervision.

To be successful, companies also need to be Boundless in terms of looking and acting less like hierarchies and more like networks, with different growth and scaling properties. Networks gain their resilience not from the size and strength of centers or owners but from the number of nodes and the strength of the connections between them. Networks have collective identities. In addition, companies need to start working more closely with their business ecosystems in order to create systemic, innovative solutions to meet their customers' current and future needs.

To be successful, companies also need to be Boundless in terms of their awareness. Companies need to be situationally aware, sensitive, and responsive to changing conditions and customer needs. And, more than that, their ability to sense and respond must be fast, frictionless, and continuous.

But even situational awareness by itself is no longer enough. Today's company needs to be "horizonally aware" as well. Horizonal awareness means being connected to the larger world beyond the immediate here and now. Companies need to be able to see further down the road in exactly the same way that an autonomous car can be aware of conditions anywhere along its journey so it can actively anticipate and avoid obstacles—all because of its global as well as local connectedness.

And, to be successful, companies also need to be Boundless in terms of their scalability. They need new ways to manage their resources.

And they need to learn to manage their technology resources—meaning AI, robots, smart devices of all types—as *coworking* with their human counterparts.

This then is the Boundless paradigm: a business model designed to do the following:

- Achieve next-level, shared success,
- Realized by resources that are individually empowered to be autonomous, connected, and mobile, and
- That are collectively organized to be integrated, distributed, and continuous.

It's a new way to think about how experiences should feel, about what products should do, and about how companies and institutions should organize and operate—especially in relation to the world and our place in it.

We are obviously not entirely alone in sensing this shift from siloed organizations to Boundless ones. The dissatisfaction with silos has been a common topic across industries for years if not decades. Stocks and flows is a core concept within economics, and visionaries have previously pointed to the need for a more flow-oriented mindset. Therefore, we're confident that we're heading in a worthwhile direction. Even so, we were surprised and thrilled to see the Accenture 2023 research report on "Total Enterprise Reinvention" with its key takeaway that "Reinvention is boundaryless and breaks down organizational silos" (Sweet et al., 2023, p. 10). We agree!

We are excited to share it with you and we are grateful for your gift of time and interest.

Boundless

Introduction

Boundless: A New Mindset
for Unlimited Business Success

"At times like these, it's easy to feel overwhelmed by the scale of the challenges we face, and the speed of each new crisis. But many complex problems have simple solutions. Sometimes you just need to decide to do something. Sometimes you just have to show up with a sandwich or some warm rice and beans."
—Chef José Andrés, World Central Kitchen

Before 2010, Chef José Andrés was best known for being one of the great chefs of the world, having trained in his native Spain at El Bulli, the restaurant widely considered the best in the world at that time, a pioneer in molecular cuisine and still considered one of the most influential and important restaurants ever, before opening his own restaurants in the US. His cuisine was, and largely still is, what we might call *high end* or *haute* cuisine, attracting a relatively affluent clientele to his highly regarded restaurants. But watching the Hurricane Katrina disaster unfold on the TV one night, he was struck by scenes at the New Orleans Superdome where hundreds of newly homeless people were sheltered but without any obvious signs of activity from relief organizations or volunteers. It was this inactivity that drove him to fly to Haiti in the aftermath of the earthquake there, with no plan, no team, only a credit card and a deep desire to act, to do something to help.

That experience led Chef José Andrés to create World Central Kitchen (WCK); to respond to humanitarian, climate, and community crises in the US and around the world and provide food relief to the local people directly affected by them. And that accomplishment by itself is worth recognizing and celebrating. But for us it's not only what WCK has and continues to achieve that is so remarkable, it's how they do it.

Our traditional relief mindset would tell us that we need to feed as many people as possible for as little as possible. Our priorities would be to produce high volumes at low unit cost, using centralized commissaries (food factories) and a volunteer workforce to squeeze as many meals out per donor dollar as possible. These meals would then be airlifted or otherwise transported to a safe place within the affected area and handed out to the affected population from that location.

WCK, however, uses a radically different approach, a new model for disaster relief as they themselves call it. They pay local restaurants, food trucks, and other related providers to source, cook, and provide food for their communities in need. Although significantly more expensive per meal, all the donor money goes straight to the local economy to help it recover faster rather than bypassing it with external services. In this way they help devastated communities recover and establish resilient food systems. By April 2021, in the year since COVID-19 had effectively shut down the hospitality industry, they had distributed $150 million to local restaurants, enabling them to stay open, their staff members to be paid, and their paychecks to support other local businesses.

The importance of this cannot be overstated. By engaging with the affected community members themselves and making them a core part of the relief, Chef Andrés and his team change the communities' perceptions of themselves. Rather than being powerless victims, they are enabled to be part of the solution, to act and to build their own resilience for the future. Their dignity, identity, and culture are never taken from them in the name of assistance. They become the heroes in their own story, and Chef is always at pains to point the credit back at them.

Not only do they mobilize local people and honor their autonomy and enable them to build their own resilience but also they honor their tradition and culture. They do this by the simple act of listening and observing. When Chef Andrés first flew out to Haiti and leaped straight into preparing food for the locals, he saw women watching him with some dissatisfaction. He realized that he was cooking food in the way that he knew, not in the way that they were used to, and that he needed to respect their local traditions to provide food that would be comforting to them and not just to deliver necessary calories. From that moment on he has approached all the situations that he and his team respond to with respect and empathy for the local people and their cultures, and with an open mind, a beginner's mindset about what will be needed on the ground, and he comes to listen. As he has said, somewhat poetically: "The emergency has this amazing way to speak to you, you only have to listen. If you are with boots on the ground, you can listen. You can listen to the situation, you can listen to the wind, you can listen to the waves, you can listen to the people."

Speed and responsiveness is another key feature of WCK. They aim to be among the very first responders to crises and to have boots on the ground preparing and delivering food, even if it's only sandwiches, on the first day they're there. It has no single template that they apply uniformly wherever help is needed, instead responding in each case to whatever is needed and whatever resources are available. But, as a general rule, they are able to move fast because they need minimum infrastructure, activating local resources wherever possible and working with whatever is available on site. And this approach not only increases their speed of response but also enables them to scale their efforts. Scale is as important to them as it is to any for-profit business, but they scale through the network, through the ecosystem, not through their own organization and their own resources. By scaling through the network they have access to far more resources than they could ever own and control.

"The way I see it, right now with World Central Kitchen I have the biggest, most powerful network of hardware in the history of mankind," Chef Andrés said. "Because, in my eyes, every kitchen is already ours. And every car. And every boat. And every helicopter. Every cook is part of our army, even if they don't know it yet . . . I don't say that openly, because people will think I'm crazy. It's just the way I see it: We are the biggest organization in the history of mankind. Even if we only have 75 people on payroll" (Martin, 2022).

With this "biggest organization in the history of mankind" WCK can deliver more than 1 million meals per day and can operate globally and locally.

The story of WCK incorporates many of the issues that are the top priorities for CEOs and other leaders across our businesses, industries, and regions. Scale is one. Income is obviously another. Although WCK is not dependent on revenue, it is still dependent on money coming into the organization to fund their efforts. Here, too, Chef Andrés has been very successful, using mobile technologies not just to communicate with his team and others but also to communicate with all of us, bringing us close, in near real time, to the disasters and the people themselves, and in doing so attract significant donor money, most notably a $100 million donation from Jeff Bezos. Again, not bad for a 70-person team.

And let's not forget that Chef Andrés is a successful business person in his own right. He runs a successful for-profit business, the José Andrés Group, in one of the most ruthlessly unforgiving industries there is, where about 60% of restaurants fail in their first year and about 80% fail within five years of opening (Kimmel, n.d.), and where COVID-19 forced chefs and restaurateurs the world over to deal with the possibility of having no customers for a year or more. The hospitality world can be an inhospitable place, but Chef understands the importance of making a profit. It's not something he hides or is ashamed of. In fact, profitability is one of his company's five core values, along with authenticity, innovation, passion, and service. But again, his mindset is different. As he describes it, "We must sustain our business in order to continue to be a successful employer and a strong pillar in the industry. *Profitability leads to possibility*" (italics our own).

Profitability in conventional terms was the purpose of business. Making a profit for the shareholders is still regarded as the primary goal of a public company. But in this new mindset profit takes on a different role, one that is more about opportunity and possibility. Profit is no longer the destination of the journey, it is the battery charge that enables the company to keep journeying and in doing so to uncover new possibilities.

Change in *n*-Dimensions

These are no longer simply uncertain or turbulent times. We've gone beyond that. Our businesses now face change in multiple dimensions, where conditions exist that make the status quo no longer tenable, where we're no longer able to simply ride things out and wait and see. Some of this change is predictable and/or cyclical, some is not. Some is trend-driven or "faddish," some is much longer term. And collectively they affect all areas of business and life in general. They are not going to go away, the dust is not going to settle, at least not for the foreseeable future. And there is no blue pill.

The first obvious dimension is **technological**. Technological advances are here to stay, and we see them continue to accelerate with no clear end in sight—digitization of mostly everything, electrification of mostly all forms of transportation and travel, artificial intelligence, robotics and machine learning, autonomous vehicles, additive manufacturing, web3 and cryptocurrencies, NFTs, digital identities and DAOs (decentralized autonomous organizations), off-planet exploration and development, and way more, all in their early stages of development. This will drive massive changes to society and may well prove to be as world changing as the 50 years between 1875 and 1925, which represented an explosive surge in invention, including electricity generators (both AC and DC), the electric lightbulb, the turbine, telephone, television, radio, car, and airplane. This spells huge opportunities for those companies that can align their capabilities, operating models, and mindsets on these technologies, and near certain death for those who can't.

The second dimension is about **capabilities**. Individuals have far greater power(s) and choices than they've ever had, largely driven by technological advances, and they're far quicker at absorbing and adopting those that they find useful than large organizations can. As customers and consumers they're more demanding, more hungry for innovation and experience, and more driven by values as well as value.

And as employees the same is true, especially employees of the future, who will be joining the workforce with years of mobile technology use as digital natives, with comparatively little interest in fitting the corporate mold, and with greater social awareness than many of our current generation of leaders. Companies can no longer afford to treat their customers as a mass market, or their employees as resource units. Meanwhile, we know that our communities are hungry for greater involvement from our businesses and we expect this trend to continue.

The third is about **crisis**. A crisis is a time of danger and difficulty, and yet a time of opportunity and possibility as well. It is a time that requires decisiveness and bold action. It is a time when the old ways of doing things come under attack and cannot be counted on to guide us out of danger. So we need not only decision-making and action taking but also new kinds of thinking and responding. The word *crisis* originally referred to a decisive point in an illness that could lead to recovery or to death. So a crisis can be a turning point. In Japanese the word points directly toward this duality to both the danger and the opportunity that a crisis brings. This new world is full of such moments, moments that seem to be dangerous but also ripe with opportunities for innovation, for breaking new ground, and for resilience. But with a twist. Resilience in crisis is not about bouncing back to a previous state, to a former status quo or to "normality." It's all about bouncing forward to a better new way of being and doing.

We are seeing crises in individual sectors, for instance, currently in the banking sector, and more broadly and more long term in society and the environment. The loss of life from COVID-19 was, and continues to be, tragic and heartbreaking for so many people around the world, and the long-term impact of the imposed isolation on many other people's health, especially emotional and psychological, has yet to be fully known. But there is much to be learned both about our old ways of working and about our response to the crisis that can set our businesses and our communities up for greater resilience and success in the future, whether we are visited by further pandemics or not. But an even greater disaster perhaps, one that we have largely ignored until recently when we really do seem to have arrived at its turning point—its crisis—is the health of many of the world's natural ecosystems and environments. For companies it will not be enough to focus on just one area of their operations to turn green. This will require not just a whole-company response but a connected-company response.

In each of these dimensions (and in others we have missed or that are just now brewing or that are to come at a later stage), our leaders and our businesses need to act. And not just to act, but to act differently. To do that they need to have a different mindset to the one that was so successful for so long and that has shaped all of our industries.

We know we're not the first to point out that leaders need to think and act differently. Business leaders are regularly advised in well-meaning articles, books, and presentations to "think differently" if they want to be successful in the digital age. The idea that thinking differently is the key to future success has been popular at least since Einstein who, talking about the potential impact of the atomic bomb on the future of humanity, was quoted as saying, "A new type of thinking is essential if mankind is to survive and move toward higher levels" ("Atomic Education Urged by Einstein," 1946).

More prosaically, but even more famously, Apple challenged us all to "Think Different" in its iconic marketing campaign that launched in September 1997. Narrated by the actor Richard Dreyfuss, the original TV advertisement celebrates "the crazy ones, the misfits, the rebels, the troublemakers—the round pegs in the square holes. The ones who see things differently." With imagery of some of the 20th century's most visionary figures, the ad clearly connects Steve Jobs to Einstein himself and other iconic leaders, laying the groundwork for Apple itself and the users of its products to imagine themselves in the same tradition of creativity, innovation and, well, difference.

The message still feels relevant some quarter of a century later because the world has changed significantly in the time that it has taken for many or even most of these leaders to climb from their entry-level positions to the top of their companies and institutions. During that period digital technology has dramatically altered the business landscape. In particular, it has fundamentally altered the power dynamic between the large and the small, between big business and startups, between companies and consumers. Technology democratizes capabilities and removes barriers to entry.

So "think differently" is good advice. But it doesn't go nearly far enough. Because it never tells the leaders how exactly they're meant to think and act differently. Which is a problem. Because it's more or less impossible to think differently if you don't have either a model for understanding how you currently do think or a new one to replace it.

The Boundless Model

So why did we start this book with Chef José Andrés and WCK? Quite simply because he's shown a new way to succeed in his chosen field, a way in which success is shared by all stakeholders. He is bringing a way of thinking and acting that is different to traditional models in nearly every respect and that is still able to have enormous impact and do incredible good. And we highlighted him and his team because his chosen field is an extreme version of the multidimensional change that we just described, namely, a societal crisis. Throughout this book we will provide other examples of this model, examples from across industries and across regions to show that it is just as relevant to other types of change and disruption as it is to crisis. This is a book about achieving next-level success, regardless of the field in which that success is sought. But we will come back to Chef Andrés again toward the end of the book because he and his team are as good an example of the Boundless model and principles as there could possibly be.

So this is not a book about the exceptional efforts required to respond to times of exception, but rather it's about a new way to normalize the efforts required to respond to increasingly normal circumstances in which change is coming at us from all directions and often at once. It's a model for bouncing forward.

Our approach in this book is to introduce this new model in enough detail so that thinking differently about the future of business becomes less abstract and can be turned into actionable insights. Specifically, we aim to provide those leaders with a way to understand and transform how they think about growing and scaling their business and about how they define and measure success as they are faced with both danger and opportunity.

We'll start by introducing a way to think about how the majority of companies, organizations, and institutions currently manage themselves and their resources. And what we attempt to show you in Chapter 1 is that the vast majority of companies and institutions across all sectors and industries, despite their obvious differences, share the exact same model when it comes to how they manage their resources to increase their value. This model is based on the desire for structural stability, where *resilience = resistance*. We call this model the *siloed organization*, or the *silo mindset*.

Silos are the organizational constructs that we are all too well aware of but that don't seem to go away however much we claim to want to smash them. Our belief is this: that silos, far from being the failure of management that we all say they are, are actually the blueprint for all companies that have been successful up to this point. Silos are, of course, meant to be metaphorical, named after the agricultural buildings that store grain after harvest. The whole point of these silos is to accumulate grain from the fields and then to protect it (from the elements, predators, pests, disease, theft) and keep it in good condition for as long as necessary until demand for it is at its highest. And silos have been doing this for a very long time, in fact, for at least 10,000 years. By their very nature they are controlled environments, meaning that they control what goes into them and when, what comes out of them and when, they control their own internal operating conditions, and they control the state of the accumulated resources themselves. Silos succeed by accumulating valuable resources and then limiting access to and driving up demand for them. That's what they do.

And it turns out this isn't so metaphorical after all but actually the way nearly all companies think about their resources, whether that resource is data, money, skills and expertise, decision-making authority, raw materials, customers, or any other resource type. What chief human resource officer worth their salt would not say that their goal is to "attract, acquire, and retain the best talent"? What chief marketing or revenue officer would not say that their goal is to "attract, acquire, and retain the best customers"? What chief information or technology or security officer would not say that their goal is to "accumulate and protect customer data"? What chief legal officer would not say that their goal is to "protect the company's IP?" Every single leader knows that their influence or power is directly related to the value of the resources under their control. So they're not going to give them away for free. No one values free stuff.

This is what a silo is, both organizationally as well as physically. It is something that controls resources and access to them. And the reason that silos don't go away is that we have all been exposed to them just as the way things are from childhood. Our classrooms are physical silos, our division of knowledge into different disciplines, departments, and schools is silo thinking; our belief that education is about the individual accumulation of knowledge and that sharing knowledge can be "cheating" is silo thinking; our testing, examining, grading, and scoring is all silo mindset. The accumulation and protection of valuable resources becomes second nature.

The problem with the silo mindset is that it was created for structural stability or even rigidity. By their nature, silos create delay. They are intended precisely to protect their resources and generate demand for them by controlling and even limiting access to them. That's why they can be so frustrating, because they withhold resources from us that we feel should be freely available. This has been a persistent problem for larger organizations with multiple divisions, departments, products, and locations. Orchestrating the flow of resources across silo boundaries to achieve results that benefit the organization can become exponentially more difficult with the silo mindset. And although we are not saying that all silos are bad by any means, we are saying that they are a choice, not an inevitability, and that there is an alternative that works quite differently and that can have even better outcomes.

That alternative, the second model, is the Boundless organization and mindset, which is the model for how businesses could and should look if we were ever to be successful in actually demolishing our silos. A small number of pioneer organizations, WCK among them, have successfully created radically differentiated business models compared to their industry norms, establishing themselves as innovative and even disruptive leaders. They have done that by reinventing the way they manage their resources. In direct opposition to the deeply ingrained and near universally practiced principles of resource accumulation and control, they are encouraging instead the flow of those resources, including ideas and information, raw materials and finished goods, employees, and customers, even by-products and waste. In doing so, they have demonstrated the viability of a new route to success and a more sustainable business paradigm for the future. We have called this paradigm *Boundless*.

All Boundless organizations, regardless of industry, region, or size, share some core characteristics or what we think of as the Boundless design principles.

They all **connect** to the outside world more deeply than their silo counterparts. They are connected to their partner ecosystems, to their customers, to their communities. At the simplest level they deeply listen to their customers and are organized to be responsive to them. At the most complex they are working hand in hand with local businesses and other community partners, extending their reach through empowering them.

They are **distributed** or decentralized, meaning that they are able to serve their customers and communities locally rather than requiring their customers to come to them. They are equipped and organized to enable working from anywhere and they are ready to exploit current and future waves of technologies that extend their reach outward.

Internally, their systems are **integrated** to enable sharing of data and other resources across the organization and to support end-to-end customer journeys and relationships. Their employees are all aligned on a core purpose, vision, and values that keep them working toward the same goals even when they're working from anywhere.

They believe in **autonomy** so that their employees feel that they have agency and meaning in their work, their customers feel empowered, and their communities become self-sufficient and resilient. They embrace artificial intelligence, machine learning and autonomy, and other technologies that become partners in their work and missions, not just tools.

They design for movement and **mobility**, literally and figuratively. Their workplaces are designed to promote movement; their business processes ensure that data, product, and decision-making all flow; their employees are encouraged and enabled to move physically for health and to have mobility in their careers. They enable mobility for their customers as well, ensuring that they can be supported wherever they are, and they drive core business communications and processes through mobile technologies by default.

They practice **continuity** in their processes so improvements and innovations are introduced to the business on a frequent basis.

They make decisions more quickly to enable teams and initiatives to flow more smoothly. They apply Agile techniques to their digital processes, and apply analogous practices to other processes including sales, marketing, finance, and others. Through continuity they are set up for speed when speed is necessary and for responsiveness more broadly.

And last but by no means least, they are driven in all decisions, processes, experiences, and so on to enable **shared success**. Profit is important to them because it enables them to keep having impact, but they design for customer, employee, partner, community, and environment success first and enjoy the benefits of doing so. They believe in win–win–win effects or non-zero-sum games.

This book is a guide to this new paradigm, this new model of thinking and acting. It offers a new paradigm for success in a time of multidimensional change and even of crisis. It is a story of leaders like Chef José Andrés and others across many different industries and regions who have shown us possibilities and opportunities, ways to bounce forward. It is also a story of human experiences, technological advances, and business models that have emerged from this Boundless mindset. And it's not just a collection of stories but also an overstory, a set of principles, briefly introduced, that they all share even though they may not have articulated them as such.

This book is intended for two audiences. Our first audience is designers, strategists, and leaders, and we hope that they will use the principles to help them in their own work of shaping the future. And our second audience is more general, meaning anyone who is interested in understanding aspects of the business world at a macro level, and who is interested in challenging the status quo at their own company or institution or in their own thinking. It is therefore intended to be of equal interest to a leader or to a practitioner. That said, it is not a "how-to" guide. Although we provide as many examples as possible to illustrate the Boundless organization it will require the reader to put the effort in toward applying the concepts to their own company. For those who might ask us where to start, the answer is to start with your own worldview. What do you believe about resources, control, and success? Only once you know that for yourself will you be able to take the next step with others.

★ ★ ★

Our book, then, is an exploration of both silos as the incumbent and highly dominant paradigm of business success and Boundless organizations as an emergent paradigm for the future. It is our intent to show that business models based on analogies and principles of structural stability—the silos of our story—are ill-prepared for the crises that will inevitably stress test them, but those that are based on principles of inherent instability—Boundless organizations—will find the opportunities that exist in dangerous times and will iteratively bounce forward and increase in resilience.

In Chapter 1 we will show how a simple idea about the centralized storage of grain over 10,000 years ago became the blueprint for the management of all types of resources, living and nonliving, physical and conceptual, ever since. We will hope to convince you that silos are, on the one hand, the foundation for nearly all the businesses that exist but that, on the other hand, despite being successful for so long, they are now increasingly the cause of business failure and that this trend will also continue going forward.

In Chapter 2 we will introduce the Boundless mindset and operating principles. We will show how being Boundless can apply equally to business operating models, technological advances, and experiences, as well as to individual behaviors and mindsets. We will contrast the principles of Boundless organizations with those of silos, showing how they lead to entirely different kinds of outcomes.

In Chapters 3 through 9 we will then discuss each of these principles in depth, demonstrating their difference from their silo counterparts. We will introduce examples from across different industries and institutions and from across different countries and continents. We will also introduce the three major themes that we see emerging in the discussion of each principle, themes that are sometimes industry-specific and other times more universal.

Finally, in Chapter 10 we will introduce the Boundless operating model.

★ ★ ★

"Water is fluid, soft, and yielding. But water will wear away rock, which is rigid and cannot yield. As a rule, whatever is fluid, soft, and yielding will overcome whatever is rigid and hard. This is another paradox: what is soft is strong."

—*Lao Tzu (McDonald, 2017)*

We all immediately recognize the silo mindset when some other department controls access to the resources we need, whether that's information, expertise, budget, extra headcount, or decision-making. But it's much less obvious that these kinds of delays and blockages are actually "features, not bugs" of the way nearly all our companies and institutions are organized. And because this way of organizing our resources is so prevalent, it is not at all obvious that there could be an alternative. The business world we all inhabit seems to be just the way things are. After all, it has worked this way for a very long time.

But in a world where forces of change are the norm rather than the exception, and where responsiveness, innovation, and fluidity are the necessary responses to those forces, the silo is simply not going to work any longer. It is becoming a victim of its own success. A new way of thinking and organizing is needed, a new paradigm is needed for anyone and any organization that wants to seize opportunity from danger. In place of going it alone, we need connectedness; in place of accumulation, we need flow; in place of control, we need autonomy. In short, we all need a Boundless mindset.

So if you believe, as we do, that our companies can no longer get to the next level using the same mindset that has gotten us to our current state, then this book is for you. You may see these times as crises, you may see them as opportunities, but in either case our book is intended to offer you a path forward to a more successful and holistically resilient future. What are you going to get out of this book? Three main things:

- First, you should have a new way of understanding, at a macro level, how your own organization works, your status quo or as-is state. You should be able to recognize where the silo mentality is strongest, to identify your orthodoxies, the practices that are "just the way we do things," and to recognize those orthodoxies as choices, not necessities or absolutes.
- Second, you should have an entirely new lens for thinking about how your organization could work, a vision for your company or your institution as a Boundless version of itself, a future or to-be state, driven by a redefinition of what success needs to look like in this new decentralized, digital-first, but at-risk, world.
- Third, you should have the beginnings of a new vocabulary and set of models for reimagining the business. Although this book is not an instructional guide, it should provide enough examples in the real world and enough conceptual frameworks to set you on your way.

So let's start our Boundless journey together.

1

Silos Kill!

The Limitations of "Acquire and Retain"

"Some influences stand out like a landmark and leave a traceable legacy with evident heirs. But the most profound influences soak into the cultural landscape like rain and nourish everyday consciousness. Such an influence is likely to go undetected, for it comes to seem the way things have always been, the natural or even the only way to look at the world."

—Rebecca Solnit (1999, p. 85)

Our businesses are organized to achieve economies of scale. The remarkable thing is that they nearly all go about it in the same way. They acquire and centralize as many resources as they can; then manage, process, and improve them as uniformly as possible, getting the most amount of work done for the least possible direct cost to themselves. We call this the silo mindset and it has been extraordinarily successful. But this model has other costs that are only recently being recognized, such as unresponsiveness to customer needs, overproduction and other forms of waste, and externalities or costs that are borne not by the silo itself but by the broader system of which it is a part. In other words, the silos model is fast becoming a victim of its own success.

Consider the following headlines: "How to Smash a Silo" (Fenn, 2023), "Why Data Silos Are Bad for Business" (Scott, 2018), "The Negative Impact of Business Process Silos on Productivity" (ISS Group, 2021), and "Smash Silos to Improve Cross Functional Communication" (Kessinger, 2017). Every few months another well-meaning article urges us to destroy the silos in our business—siloed teams and departments, siloed data and systems, siloed processes and practices—for the continued well-being of our firms. So why are they so prevalent, not just in the business world but also in academia—where their presence is just as criticized and just as ubiquitous (e.g., Friedlander, 2022)—and in education and in health care (e.g., Kahn, 2020), and just about anywhere else we care to look?

One particular problem with silos concerns not just the fact that we don't get (all) the resources we need to do our job when we need them, but, even more so, that those resources are being deliberately withheld by the department or business or operating unit managing them. In those situations, the "guilty" department or unit or group is acting as a silo. Worse yet, that withholding of valuable resources is not an anomaly or an unintentional consequence but actually *exactly* how silos are intended to work. And our businesses are organized in the same way with the same intent. They acquire valuable resources, create economies of scale, and release those resources only when they're most needed and they can be exploited most fully.

This description doesn't just apply to knowledge, or to grain, or even to missiles. It's how we manage and increase the value of nearly all kinds of resources—and if we look closely enough, we'll find silos of one kind or another, albeit thinly disguised under different names, just about everywhere. We accumulate gold and seeds and other strategic reserves in vaults, water behind dams, money in banks, patients in waiting rooms, students in classrooms, employees in cube farms, pigs and chicken in factory farms, and so on almost endlessly. Silos are part of this long and deep tradition of resource management at scale that works for the resource owner—and often for no one else.

Silos are so prevalent because they have worked, at least for the silo owners, for a very long time. They're very effective at a particular kind of scaling: generating the most value out of their resources. They're optimized to scale resource productivity.

There is an interesting and important difference between the way we make the first of a kind—a prototype, a one-off, an experiment (successful or not)—and the way we make the nth of a kind. More specifically, perhaps there's a difference between how we organize to create or process or build one instance of a thing and how we organize to create or process or build many instances of that thing.

When we build or make a new concept or prototype, or when we set out to teach one child, or when we plant a vegetable garden for our family, or when we do just about anything on a small or individual basis, our focus is almost entirely on that one thing: that prototype or child or vegetable. We invest all our energy, time, money, and effort directly on the object of our endeavors, with little thought to the conditions and context within which we're operating.

But when we try to do the same thing on a large scale—whether that's the mass development of software, or the mass production of a widget, or the mass education of the nation's children, or the mass feeding of the population—our focus and our investment in time, effort, and money changes entirely. What we spend our resources on is the infrastructure: the factory floor, the school, the office, the farm; the tools and equipment; the situation, context, and conditions; the administration, the training, the management; the upkeep and maintenance; the marketing and advertising; the hiring of all the above skills; the legal fees. Unfortunately, all these resources can deplete if not entirely absorb all the time, effort, or money we had intended to dedicate to the object of our endeavors: the individual widget, child, animal, or vegetable. In short, the more units we make of a thing, the less we spend on each unit and the more we spend on infrastructure.

This is, of course, what's known as scaling. To achieve the most efficient processes, we minimize variability, reduce costs of management, make efficient use of space, increase volume.

Silo Principles

All silos work in essentially the same way; they share one overarching principle: how they define and measure success. In brief: *silos measure success by the value they extract from their resources.* This typically but not always produces profit. In order to achieve that success, they typically exercise as much control as possible: over their resources, their inputs and outputs, and their internal environment. We have identified 12 common ways in which they do that.

Resource Control

Accumulation. As we have already discussed, silos accumulate and concentrate resources to make them easier to manage, be they corporate databases or strategic reserves, livestock facilities or prisons, business units or academic schools or disciplines. This accumulation also has the effect of drawing attention to the resources while providing only limited access to them—which makes them seem more valuable.

Isolation. Silos separate resource units from one another to limit potential contagion and to discourage interaction between them, especially when it would be hazardous for those resources to be too closely situated to one another. From grain explosions to oil fires, to fights among spectators at sporting events and the ready spread of diseases in crowds, proximity can be dangerous—and so control is facilitated by keeping resources apart.

Immobilization. Silos situate resource units in the smallest possible cells both to isolate and to limit their movement for ease of management and space efficiency. Examples include individual desks for students to cubicles for employees, animal pens, prison cells, airplane seating, and so on. In other settings, consumers are often brought to a standstill in order to be processed, such as at checkout lines, waiting rooms, highway toll plazas, and call center wait times and holds.

Dependency. Silos need to provide support systems to their resources. Farms have to nourish their livestock and plants to keep them healthy, whereas corporations might have canteens, gyms, or laundry services to keep their employees productive.

Input/Output Control

Decoupling. The resources in silos have been extracted from their "natural" environment, stripped of their support systems, and cleansed of impurities. The goal is to hold only the "essence" that makes the resource valuable. In school this means educating a child's brain at the expense of their body and spirit, and in business it means capitalizing on an employee's brain or hands at the expense of their body and spirit—in brief, productivity without wellness. This decoupling can also mean decontextualizing data to make it easier to analyze—at the expense of potentially lessening its meaning.

Monotypism. Silos are specialist environments that only accept and store one kind of resource. They are not mixed-use storage facilities; they are "specific" not "generic." Hence our businesses are organized by function, our universities by discipline, our high schools by age, our farms by product, our prisons by security classification, and our customers by persona or segment.

Standardization. Silos are standards based. They either accept resource units of only one grade or size or quality or age—or they segregate/compartmentalize them accordingly; thus, even within the monotypism, quality or capability is assessed. For example, businesses tend to have hiring criteria that include a mandatory required level of academic achievement and "previous industry experience." "Fit" is valued and sameness is sought, no matter how loudly the desire for diversity is declared.

Batching. Silos control the timing, quality, and quantity of resources and/or final product that they input, process, and/or release at any one time. They tend to favor fewer releases and more resources per release at predetermined, seasonal, or annual cadences. In education this means annual enrollment and graduation ceremonies of all students in the class at the same time. In business this means annual planning and budgeting, seasonal marketing campaigns and product launches, and annual hiring. Previously in computing this included overnight batch processing of records instead of real-time processing; today this refers to the practice of releasing systems only on completion of all required functionality.

Environment Control

Exclusion. Silos, both organizational and physical, are built to keep their resources within their walls and to keep everything and everyone else out. There is a clear distinction between insiders and outsiders, between the company and its vendors and suppliers, customers and competitors. Security measures in office buildings, employee passes, VPNs, company policies, lawsuits against intellectual property theft all reinforce the hardened division between the inside and out.

Simplicity. The insides of silos are designed as uniform "cells," compartmentalizing the space and creating a standardized environment. Offices, classrooms, and hospital rooms are all viewed as functional spaces, blank backdrops against which work is done—not as part of the experience itself. The cell is considered the ideal environment in which resource productivity can be maximized.

Variable management. Silos carefully manage and manipulate the dimensions or variables of light, heat, oxygen, nitrogen, water, nutrients, cycles, and so on. The most sophisticated silos can create particularly suitable conditions—either for maximal growth, for example, in vertical farms, or for retarding growth, for example, to keep produce in good condition before being released into the market.

Dumping. Silos flush or discard waste, by-products, and/or defects—anything that might be toxic to its resources—to the outside without regard for external contamination or pollution. And in contrast to the way silos' successes are batched, these failures tend to be dealt with individually and immediately: whether it's factories dumping physical waste, schools expelling rule breakers, or businesses firing problematic employees. And because the silos' managers don't bear the costs of these and other externalities, as a result, the price of the finished goods or services is held artificially low.

★ ★ ★

To be clear, these principles do not describe the types of improvement or processing that is unique to different organizations and industries. The work of a school is obviously different from that of a hospital or an office or a farm. And yet, the ways these students, patients, employees, and livestock are managed are strikingly similar, and managers often follow these principles, even if unconsciously.

As you can see, silos aren't just physical structures, holding grain, for example. Silos have become a way that most of us think about the world and experience the world and go out to perform in the world. We spend our childhood and adolescence being organized at school in this way: being taught that the acquisition and retention of knowledge is valuable and being rewarded for demonstrating our ability to do so individually—or being punished for sharing that knowledge inappropriately, which we call cheating.

Silo logic then is a way of thinking about the world that embraces control, homogeneity, "inside-ness" or interiority, fit, isolation, and withholding. Silo logic favors the delineation of territory and the control of boundaries. It believes that the resources inside the silo are considered of high value to those outside the silo, and it gains its power, wealth, and sense of self-worth from doing everything it can to persuade outsiders accordingly.

Impact and Reach of Silos

Our discussion so far may seem rather abstract or of only peripheral relevance and importance, but let's be really clear about the scope and reach of this silo mindset:

- More than 90% of all the meat we eat comes from confinement or "factory" farms, where animals are typically held in pens that limit movement and contact between them—thus reducing the cost of feeding, treating, and otherwise processing them (e.g., Foodindustry.com, 2022).
- In the US, well over 95% of all corn and soybeans, the two most widely grown crops by far, are produced on conventional farms that practice monoculture. More than 90% of all other cereal grains, fruits, and vegetables are also produced on conventional farms (e.g., Bialik & Walker, 2019).
- Approximately 90% of all children in the US are educated in a traditional public school setting with a teacher delivering the same content and instructions to 20 or more students simultaneously in

conventional classrooms organized by age and/or subject. The
remaining 10% mostly attend private schools, many of which are
organized similarly (e.g., Bouchrika, 2022).

- Before 2020, only 6% of the entire US workforce worked from
home; the vast majority worked from traditional workplace
settings. Approximately 70% of all white-collar workers worked
full-time in traditional office settings, complete with cubicles
and management offices, and had never worked from home
(e.g., Goldberg, 2022).

- Approximately 2 million or so people in the US are incarcer-
ated. All are classified and allocated to the appropriate prison
type (with five levels of security: minimal, low, medium, high,
and administrative) based on the severity of their crime, and
their movement and contact with others is strictly controlled
based on that categorization (e.g., Sawyer & Wagner, 2023).

- The vast majority of chief marketing officers would say that
their job is to acquire and retain customers. The vast majority
of chief human resources officers would say that their job is to
attract and retain top talent. Most other executives would
describe their job in very similar ways based on their most
valuable resources. With very few exceptions, chief executive
officers have profit and growth as their top priorities.

- As much as 65% of companies collect so much information
that they're unable to fully categorize or analyze it (e.g., Thales
Group, 2018).

Problems with the Silo Mindset

We can expect silos to continue well into the future, and of course
they are not all "bad." Silos increase the value of the resources under
their control. The beneficiary of the increase in value is conventionally the shareholder, and the value itself is measured in terms of

margin between the cost of improvement and the price attained in the market for that improvement.

The value to the customer and to business partners is of secondary importance, and the impact of the companies' operations on the well-being and success of the resources themselves—and on that of the communities and ecosystems within which they operate—has traditionally been of little to no concern.

But in this new era of accelerating technological innovation; of increasingly more empowered, informed, and demanding customers and employees alike; and of growing societal concern for the impact of our modes and means of production on the environment and the planet more broadly, the silo mindset is steadily becoming less tenable. Here are some direct consequences of organizing as silos:

Silos can lead to a lack of responsiveness to current customer needs and anticipation of their future or changing ones. Companies and institutions with strong silos can be slow to respond to customer needs or market conditions because information, expertise, and other resources are hoarded rather than shared. Decision-making gets delayed and is then potentially misinformed by incomplete, out-of-date, and even conflicting data from different parts of the organization. Innovation is often stifled, since ideas generated in one part of the organization can be routinely ignored or dismissed by other parts—and those ideas that do make it through are often unrecognizable by the time they reach their final form, having been subjected to compromises along the way.

Silos are liable to overproduction, one of the common side effects of batching and one of the seven types of waste—collectively known as *muda*—identified in the famed Toyota Production System (Ohno, 1988). In fact, out of all seven types, overproduction is often regarded as the worst type of waste because it creates an inability to respond to changing customer needs. It creates high inventory levels of products that no one wants that are then stuffed into the pipeline, resulting in deep discounts, reduced revenues, and literally nowhere for new products to go—the bane of consumer goods companies everywhere.

Because of their focus on acquisition and retention, siloed companies can find themselves with massive collections of data but no clear idea about what they have or what to do with it all. Data, often inaccurate and incomplete, can be duplicated across multiple systems, making it difficult to integrate systems and provide clear end-to-end support of the customer journey.

Silos can lead to a lack of employee engagement, autonomy, and purpose. Siloed companies, with their relentless focus on resource productivity and their traditional management-by-control approach, become unattractive places to work for people looking for greater autonomy and purpose in their work lives. Additionally, although individuals feel that they are being required to do more with less and to work faster and harder, their organizations still feel slow and incapable of change. The silos generate routine frustration and friction, waste time, disable cross-company communication and collaboration, and incentivize individual over team and collective productivity.

Silos can lead to nonexistent or poor relationships with partners, communities, and the environment. Silos create inequities or incompatibilities between those who own and control resources and those who need them. Additionally, silos are only parts of systems—they're not systems themselves. Optimizing for the success of the silo can compromise the overall success and well-being of the system, whether that system is a company, industry, community, or ecosystem.

Silos also tend to keep vendors and suppliers at arm's length, missing the opportunity to build ecosystem relationships with them and co-innovate on behalf of their mutual customers.

Silos can weaken, deplete, or contaminate the community or ecosystem of which they are a part by removing needed resources, dumping concentrated by-product and waste, and rendering other parts of the system ineffective. They can deplete and even exhaust finite resources, and they are often reluctant (or may not even be able) to adapt to changing system conditions and needs.

Ultimately, silos risk their own downfall by ignoring the outside world—which tends to find alternatives, substitutes, or competitive resources elsewhere.

Silos at the Extreme

Silos tend to have consequences that are commensurate with their size. The larger the silos, the greater the potential for negative impact. In her 2015 book *The Silo Effect: The Peril of Expertise and the Promise of Breaking Down Barriers*, Gillian Tett investigates the impact of the lack of information sharing—in this case between intelligence agencies leading up to 911 and among New York first responders in the immediate aftermath. Silos can have tragic consequences.

But note, these problems are not random effects, unintended repercussions, or accidental by-products of our otherwise well-meaning actions; they are inevitable outcomes of an intentional, millennia-tested model for optimal resource productivity. Nor are they niche—limited to obscure or specialized situations; on the contrary, by our estimate silo-based resource management governs at least

90% of all our industries and institutions. Nearly all our companies, universities, hospitals, schools, farms, prisons, and so on apply the same set of management principles to their resources, human and non-human alike.

So, if we truly want to smash the silos, we're going to need something much deeper than an impassioned plea. We're going to need an alternative—a whole new business paradigm, in fact—for all types of silos. That alternative is Boundless.

2 | The Anti-Silo

The Boundless Alternative

"In the beginner's mind there is no thought, 'I have attained something.' All self-centered thoughts limit our vast mind. When we have no thought of achievement, no thought of self, we are true beginners. Then we can really learn something. The beginner's mind is the mind of compassion. When our mind is compassionate, it is boundless."

—*Shunryu Suzuki (2011)*

Boundless is a redefinition of success, one that extends way beyond the traditional or siloed definition. Boundless companies, experiences, and mindsets have a compass that points outward toward customers, partners, and communities rather than inward toward their own processes. They aim to spread themselves out into those communities rather than distance and separate themselves from it. To be Boundless is to reorient ourselves, to use technology to reach out, to connect with each other, our customers, our business ecosystems, our communities, and our environment. Boundless is what you get when you bring together the power of networks and flow—an entirely new paradigm for next-level success in this increasingly connected, increasingly smart, and increasingly at-risk world.

In Chapter 1, we argued that organizational silos are not what they seem. They are not anomalies or aberrations or management gone bad. They are not a recent malaise or by-product of the digital era. They are in fact just everyday examples of an approach to resource management that has been successful for millennia and that pervades all industries and all regions.

So even though they do cause all the problems that we attribute to them—including wasted time and increased friction, ineffective communications, untimely decision-making, unresponsiveness, and loss of business—they're nonetheless ubiquitous.

We need a new model, one that extends success to a much broader set of stakeholders, minimizes waste and maximizes responsiveness, and enables our companies to thrive in an era of constant change.

The Boundless Principles

Boundless is that new model, a different way to think about how companies and institutions should organize and operate, about how customer experiences should feel, about what products should do, and about the world and our place in it.

Because silo-based resource management is so ubiquitous across our industries and institutions, alternative approaches are relatively rare. Some industries, however, have already started rethinking their approach to resource management and have recognized the value in setting their resources in motion and transforming them in flow. Manufacturing in particular has long advocated for flow, and approaches like just-in-time manufacturing have existed for decades. Since the 2010s pharmaceutical companies have begun to explore in-flow production, the benefits of which we outline next.

Organizations that have implemented in-flow and Boundless solutions are typically among the most differentiated and successful players in their industry or market. And because they represent only a very small part of the whole, there is massive opportunity for transformation, including eliminating customer wait times; freeing the flow of information across and beyond the organization; utilizing flow-based energy sources such as the sun, wind, and water; and supporting customers, employees, students, individuals, and communities in their respective flows.

Boundless entities commonly disrupt industry norms and orthodoxies. Our research has found that these entities share, even if implicitly, a set of design principles that generate and guide this revolutionary business model: connection, distribution, integration, autonomy, mobility, continuity, and shared success.

These principles are not mutually exclusive, nor are they intended to be, although they are collectively exhaustive in the sense that together they explain the most salient features of any Boundless system. Not surprisingly, the principles are the exact opposites of the principles of silos. They can work for all companies, large and small, traditional and "modern," digital and analog. Better yet: we've observed that, the more companies apply these principles, the greater the transformative or even disruptive impact they tend to have.

In this section we will introduce each principle in turn. One of them, shared success, is the guiding principle behind all the others and so we will introduce that first. For each of the other principles we've also identified three emergent strategies that identify the aspects of each of the principles that are most likely to deliver the highest impact.

Guiding Principle: Shared Success

As we saw in Chapter 1, silos are designed to accumulate, defend, and protect stocks of resources so as to extract their full value. They all share one overarching principle: *they measure success by the value extracted from their resources.* That their success is measured in terms of their own outcomes is reflected in how they operate.

Boundless entities foster sustainable or regenerative practices. They make non-zero-sum game decisions, seeking success for all members of their ecosystems, environments, and communities—including themselves. And so Boundless companies measure success very differently. As we saw with Chef José Andrés in the Introduction, profit can still be a priority for Boundless organizations (at least those in the commercial sector) but only so that they can continue to enable the success of all their stakeholders, including partners, customers, employees, communities, and the environment. We call this next-level, shared success. In some sectors, agriculture in particular, the term *regenerative* is used to describe holistic approaches to farming that not only design for but also measure the well-being of all partners and rights holders, including plants, animals, and the earth itself. In other circles the term *non-zero-sum game* is used. Colloquially the expressions *win-win* or *win-win-win* reflect the idea behind shared success. It's not just organizations themselves that can be Boundless. Stakeholder experiences, products and services, organizational structures, and new business models can all be designed to achieve this goal. Regardless of industry or resource application, they nearly always produce the same win–win–win effect, reducing operational costs while simultaneously improving the customer experience and the environmental or community impact.

Connection: Sensing | Relationships | Ecosystems

Whereas silos see themselves as stand-alone entities and work to maintain the distinction between themselves and the outside world, Boundless entities recognize that they are in fact connected to that outside world, market, or ecosystem of which they are a part. We have identified three ways in which companies are becoming Boundless through their ability to connect.

The first is in companies' ability to **sense** what's happening in their environment and with all members and parts of it. They realize that their ability to be autonomous depends, perhaps counterintuitively, on being more connected than ever before. This ability is almost entirely dependent on the effective use of sensing technologies, because there are too many moving parts, too much complexity, and too much real-time data for humans to sense and make sense of them without assistance. (Having said that, the ability and willingness to listen—to listen to understand—is an essential human skill and a vital complement to sensing.)

The second way companies are becoming Boundless through their ability to connect is in their understanding of the importance of **relationships**. Successful relationships are still at the heart of all business—just as they are at the heart of all other human institutions—and yet few companies are intentional about designing for the types of relationships they want to have with their customers, employees, and partners. This is therefore an area that is ripe for innovation: we see significant need for relationship design, relationship strategy— even for relationship transformation.

The third way companies are becoming Boundless through their ability to connect is in their ability to move beyond a traditional and linear supply or value "chain" with their various vendors and suppliers and to instead build with them business **ecosystems** in which they can cocreate or co-innovate on behalf of their mutual customers.

Distribution: Decentralizing Technologies | Remote = Local | Edges > Centers

Silos create centers, taking resources out of their natural environments or local communities and accumulating them for scale. This creates an inward-facing, highly concentrated, intensive organization. By contrast, a Boundless entity is always looking outward. It's not just connected to the world—it distributes itself and its resources throughout it.

The Boundless mindset recognizes that resources can have a different impact depending on whether they are concentrated in one place or spread out. What can be harmful or difficult to assimilate en masse (such as fertilizer or data) can become easier to consume when in smaller portions that are more widely distributed. In agriculture, intensive practices give rise to extensive ones. In manufacturing and other industries, additive, networked technologies point to a future of local, small-scale production. The arrow of technology even points to a resurgence of rural communities—as far off as that may seem.

Boundless entities take advantage of, and become more like, **decentralizing technologies** that enable or will enable them to serve their customers where they are. Now, obviously older networks such as TV, radio, or the power grid also deliver resources directly to their customers, but more modern networks enable new levels of interaction between provider and consumer—such as teleconsults in health care—as well as enabling many-to-many communications and value flows. Technologies such as solar power enable consumers to feed surplus energy back to the grid, and we can expect the Internet of Things to further accelerate and amplify the flow of information across our networks.

Boundless organizations question and even reverse the traditional relationship between HQ and "remote" workers. In a connected, networked world the HQ is remote and the remote worker is local: *remote = local.* The HQ itself is no longer a center but a pump that ensures all its resources are continuously replenished to maintain efficacy. Because Boundless organizations meet and serve their customers where they are, they enable those customers to maintain their own flow.

In the connected world the company's internal hierarchy is irrelevant. Everything that is actually important to our business success and growth—namely, our customers, our partners, and our communities—is on the outside. So it's time for us to follow new metaphors. We need to learn how to be part of networks that we neither control nor own. We need to spend less time thinking like companies do and more time thinking like our customers do—which means we need to spend more time focused on the **edges**, on the outside. After all, as customers, as individuals, as families and as communities, we're all already there.

Integration: Aligned Purpose and Value/s | Orchestration + Choreography | Circularity

Boundless entities align their employees and other resources on a common mission, plan, or purpose to enable coherent and consistent actions and behaviors. Their **aligned purpose and values** drive their decision-making as well as their behaviors and communications.

In a work-from-anywhere world companies can no longer count on the org chart and the office hierarchy to manage and supervise their teams. They have to work harder than ever to support their employees' autonomy while **orchestrating** them to ensure customer needs are met and providing them with tools to **choreograph** their collective efforts. Once again, purpose and value draw the employees together in spirit even though they may be physically and geographically dispersed or distributed. Belonging is fostered through digital "decentralized nervous systems."

Integration is by no means confined to living resources. Boundless organizations use their connections with the outside world to sense and understand what's happening, and they assimilate all the inputs from their sensing mechanisms—including all their customer-facing systems—and integrate them to create a synthesized view of customer journeys and market conditions. They are responsive to their customers' current needs and can even anticipate future needs based on the end-to-end vision and understanding of those customers' journeys.

In fact, Boundless organizations aspire to move beyond end-to-end integration and instead recognize the power of end-to-start integration, or *circular* integration. This can refer to understanding the customer journey as not just one iteration of a path from awareness to use but of multiple iterations, all adding up to a dynamic relationship. And this does not just refer to customers but also to other loops, such as the journey of raw materials to end products to recycling and reuse. The term *circular economy* is sometimes used to refer to this level of resource integration and sustainability.

Autonomy: AI | Identity | Learning

In a silo, resources are stripped of all the support systems they would have enjoyed on the "outside" and are heavily controlled on the inside. The resources become dependent on the silo owner for direction and for support. They are treated as dumb. Obedience and rule-following are rewarded and more highly prized than is creativity or innovation.

Boundless entities empower their resources—primarily employees in the business world—to make decisions and act in keeping with their unified mission, plan, or purpose and with their customer success as the primary goal. They support and empower their customers' autonomy, as well as that of their employees, through their experiences, offerings, and organizational models.

AI is a vital tool across multiple industries for supporting businesses both in decision-making and in delivering customer success. And AI is the primary means by which the autonomous vehicle gets its name. As we will see in the case study of Tesla further on in this chapter, autonomy is actually made possible by connection—but it is not just the vehicle or the technology in general that enjoys its autonomy through sensing and AI. The human, previously the operator of the machine, is now freed up to do activities that may have more value added to them, or—by contrast—to do nothing at all and just relax. Meanwhile, these technologies, driven by AI, are becoming, and will become even more so, more like teammates than like tools, more like part of the company and its decision-making capabilities itself. Although we are perhaps a ways off from this being commonplace, the idea of technology becoming part of the company itself is likely to have significant implications.

A core aspect of AI that should be an inspiration to individuals and organizations is the focus on continuous learning. AI gets smarter as real-time data flows through it and its algorithms improve their accuracy. Sensing and understanding becomes an increasingly important capability for the autonomous enterprise as much as it does for an autonomous vehicle or individual human.

The importance of autonomy plays out into the world of **identity**, where individuals are beginning to assert their desire for autonomy and ownership over their online data and identity. Companies in the future are going to need to account for this new level of autonomy and identity, as well as their own. Even in an ecosystem-driven economy, should it ever happen, a company's own identity will likely be an important consideration, for inspiring individuals to choose to work for them and for inspiring customers to transact with them.

Mobility: Flow | Mobile Technologies | Environments

Flow is essential to life. Within living systems, resources are pumped to where they are needed and are refreshed on a continuous basis. Without that movement, embolisms and other blockages would stop those flows, causing death to tissue, limbs, organs, or even the whole organism.

Boundless entities are modeled closely after living systems. They mobilize their resources to enable distribution to where they are needed and to enhance their responsiveness to emerging conditions and needs. They foster individual and collective well-being through movement—literal and figurative. They extend this theme to their customers, designing experiences that enable them to stay in their flow without waiting or stopping and without friction. Movement also enables **speed**, which is the currency in the digital economy. As such, it is more or less impossible for a company to be fast if it is built on a worldview that promotes stability and control. However, note that speed is not equally applicable across all industries. For example, the Boundless model in agriculture emphasizes movement, partially because it improves the health of its animals and partially because it enables farmers to ensure that their animals enjoy and fertilize their pastures without exhausting or contaminating them. Speed is not a value to these farms.

Success in the decentralized world, in the paradigm where business serves the customer wherever they are, depends on individual **mobility**, literally and figuratively. Mobile, connected systems and products enable individuals to be effective remotely/locally. Consider the smartphone, one of the most successful products in the history of products—at least in terms of the number of people with access to one and the speed with which that access arose. The smartphone gives the user their own autonomy, connection, and mobility—and in so doing it gives them what psychologists might call optimal functioning, self-determination, or, more prosaically, the ability to live their best life.

Continuity: Process Flow | Circulation | Mindset and Language

Boundless entities are organized for continuity of operations. This doesn't mean just that the lights stay on and the infrastructure needed to support the business maintains its availability, although, of course, all of that is important. It means that value creation, value transformation, and value exchange is always happening. Products are always being developed and delivered—driven by and driving customer demand. Decisions are always being made. Information is always being shared across the organization to enable those decisions. Expertise and all other important resources are always being made available to the parts of the organization that need them, and resources are always being refreshed to ensure their usefulness and well-being.

Agile practices in software development have been a welcome alternative to traditional "waterfall" approaches. These practices are based on principles of continuous development and delivery of functionality to customers, on continuous communication, and on the connected autonomy of the development team.

Continuity in computing has been an important principle in computing ever since the advent of multiuser systems in the 1960s. Since then we have seen shifts from a few centralized mainframes to billions of distributed devices, from nightly batch windows to 24/7 online availability, from hierarchical to relational to networked data, from proprietary to open systems, from waterfall methodologies to Agile, from monolithic applications to microservices and APIs—and, potentially, from corporate ownership of customer data to individual ownership by means of the distributed web (a current initiative led by Sir Tim Berners-Lee, the "father" of the world wide web).

In most businesses, the language needed to assimilate and embrace the idea of continuity is simply missing. In Chapter 8, we'll discuss how most business metaphors are based on the ideas of physical structure, not on the ideas of movement and continuity. In program management, the metaphors of stages and gates are widespread and readily understood. The priority is on controlling projects, ideas, products in development, and so on with the explicit goal of stopping them in order to examine and assess them before letting them move forward again. We believe that we need a new set of metaphors, and chief among them would be the idea of the circulation system and the **pump**. Pumps continually move resources forward, establishing momentum as the norm, not as an exception.

We'll see continuity show up in industries as diverse as pharmaceuticals and fashion. In each case we'll see the *many + small + frequent* paradigm, where small batches of product are produced on a frequent basis, with the capacity for as much overall volume as in a traditional or conventional business but with greater flexibility and responsiveness to changing customer and market needs.

Principles in Combination

As mentioned previously, the principles are not intended to be mutually exclusive but rather fit together in different combinations. Here are four combinations that stand out to us.

The first combination is *mobility + continuity = flow.* As we discussed in the Preface, our initial focus was on stocks and flows of resources, and our earlier articles were all about flow. We were and we still are deeply interested in the relationship between flow and life, and so we use living systems as models for how companies can design for the flow of their "lifeblood." We are also interested in the fact that renewable energy sources—such as wind, wave, tide, sunlight, and heat—tend to be flow-based, and that the new electric revolution needs flow-based sources of electricity in order to be sustainable or regenerative or Boundless in full. When we use the term *flow* in this book we are thinking about this combination of principles and about the concepts of life and renewable energy. We are not using *flow* to refer directly to the psychology of optimal experience as described by

Mihály Csíkszentmihályi (1990). Even though we see the connection between flow—a state of complete immersion in an activity—and Boundlessness, for us, flow is not the "internal" experience of an individual; for us flow is primarily the continuous and collective movement of resources in a system. (To us, individual experience is more about the related concept of self-determination, as we describe next.)

The second combination is *autonomy + connection + mobility = individual self-determination*—for which we were inspired in part by professors Edward Deci and Richard Ryan. In the late 1970s at the University of Rochester in New York, Deci and Ryan developed a theory of self-actualization and motivation called self-determination theory. The most well-known aspect of their work—largely because of the best-selling book on the topic, *Drive: The Surprising Truth About What Motivates Us* by Daniel Pink in 2009—is about motivation, where they draw a distinction between intrinsic and extrinsic motivations. But of most relevance to us is the concept of the three universal psychological needs we all have for self-determination—or, more colloquially, what we need to live our best lives. According to Deci and Ryan, those needs are autonomy, relatedness, and competence.

The way we see it, any Boundless system provides the conditions for its resources (especially but not solely its living resources, like employees, students, etc.) to enjoy a high level of autonomy. It also provides for relatedness, although we use the term *connection* instead because it can connote the connections between technological resources, the connections between technological resources and humans, and the increasing synergies and decreasing differences between the former and the latter. We have left out *competence* from our definition of self-determination for the simple reason that there is no difference between the need for competence within a siloed organization and within a Boundless one; the difference is in how competence is exploited or nurtured. And we have added **mobility** to our definition because a Boundless organization intentionally puts its resources into motion.

The third combination is *distribution + integration + continuity = collective action.* We believe that any Boundless system or organization enables each individual to be self-determining while at the same time working with their human and technological teammates toward the collective goal. This takes orchestration, or direction, from the organization as well as choreography, or peer-to-peer coordination, on the part of teams and individual members. For example, let's consider an autonomous taxi company of the future. Any given taxi in the company's fleet may decide, based on its sensing functions, that it needs servicing—and so it takes itself out of circulation. That would be individual self-determination. That the fleet scheduler would then rerun its algorithm (accounting for the unavailability of one car) and give the rest of the fleet updated directions would be orchestration. And, last, the fleet on the road communicating locally with one another (as well as with all other local nonfleet traffic) to ensure they travel at the fastest collective speed possible while maintaining the smallest safe distance between them would be choreography.

Were we to add **shared success** to either the second or the third combination we'd create individual Boundlessness and collective Boundlessness, respectively, because their actions would be driven not just by their own goals but also by the desire to ensure the success of all other related parties. And combining shared success with all six principles is the definition of a Boundless system.

The Boundless Model in Action: Case Studies

These principles can be used by all organizations who wish to design their own customer experiences, offerings, and business models for transformational or even disruptive impact. We realize, however, that they may sound merely aspirational rather than practical, so we now want to discuss how they actually apply to real companies in real industries: one very traditional and one comparatively modern and technology driven.

Veta La Palma and Regenerative Agriculture

The first case study is in agriculture, our oldest industry. The Boundless model, known in the industry as regenerative agriculture, is showing the possibility of a new paradigm for feeding the world while also caring for the planet. To start, we offer visuals of siloed and Boundless systems.

Figure 2.1 shows a highly simplified ecosystem, one that could be a natural ecosystem, a community, a market, or even a company. The ecosystem is populated with several "members" belonging to three different types or species (represented by triangles, diamonds, and pentagons for the sake of simplicity). All the members are able to interact freely with each other (which can include being part of each other's food chain!) and tend to perform different but complementary functions that maintain the health and resilience of the ecosystem.

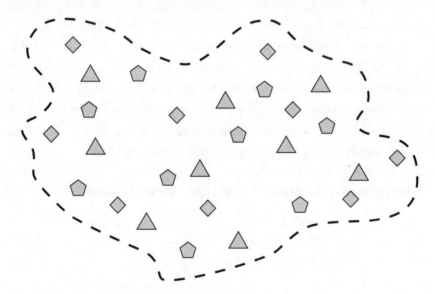

Figure 2.1 A simplified ecosystem.

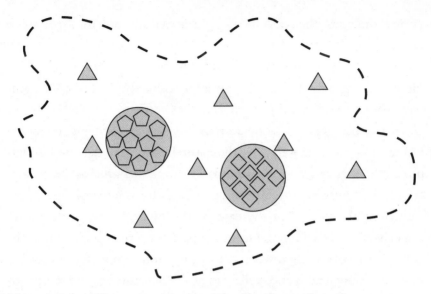

Figure 2.2 The ecosystem with silos introduced.

Figure 2.2 shows that same ecosystem but with the addition of two silos, in which are captured, separately, all the individuals of two of the member types in the ecosystem—segregating those two types at a much greater density while preventing all three types from interacting. These silos significantly threaten the overall health and resilience of the ecosystem.

What does this mean in real life? In a conventional fish farm, the fish are kept in netted cages, each one an individual silo (as in Figure 2.2). These cages are typically circular, accumulating the fish at much higher densities than they would be in the wild. This creates stress in the fish and facilitates the spread of lice and disease, which means that they have to be sprayed with chemicals, which then get into the surrounding waters. Because they're isolated by the nets from the environment at large they have to be fed, typically a diet of fish, chicken, and soy that is unnatural to them. Their excrement and other waste pollutes the environment because it is produced in a high concentration in a static location. When any of the lice, disease, or fish escape the nets the well-being of the natural aquatic ecology is endangered.

This model is directly applicable to all other forms of confinement farming, which accounts for approximately 90% of all the animal products consumed in the US (Foodindustry.com, 2022).

A Boundless system, however, in this case a regenerative farm, is modeled far more closely after the natural ecosystem depicted in Figure 2.1. Regenerative agriculture is a shining example of shared success. It is an approach to farming that cares for the well-being of the soil (or water system, in the case of aquaculture), the nurturing of the ecosystem of which the farm is a part, the stress-free living of the animals and plants themselves, the equitable pay and welfare of the workforce, the health and well-being of the customers, and the financial success of the farm itself. And not only does it care about these things but also it uses technology to measure, connect, and learn, experimenting continuously to find ways to improve. It is a combination of new and old thinking. It owes a great deal to ancestral and Indigenous thinking and practices around the interconnectedness of everything and everyone, and to their ideas that nature will provide for us if we (1) take responsibly and with gratitude and (2) reciprocate and give back generously. Regenerative farmers are often as media savvy—well, almost as savvy—as Chef Andrés is with his World Central Kitchen, educating, informing, and engaging the public in their operations, and slowly building a new, more optimistic narrative about the future of agriculture. And, in case we haven't mentioned this enough, regenerative farmers are also running viable businesses. Profit may not be their destination, but it does charge their batteries and enables them to continue their journey.

Perhaps nowhere else on earth is this more dramatically and beautifully manifested than at the Spanish fish farm Veta La Palma, brought to prominence by Chef Dan Barber in his 2010 TED Talk "How I Fell in Love with a Fish." The farm has turned the traditional agricultural model on its head. It does not isolate itself from other parts of the ecosystem but is fully *connected* with, and virtually indistinguishable from, the wider environment. In this way it fully *integrates* its fish into their ecosystem, enabling them to play their normal part in its life and be part of the overall complexity that gives the ecosystem its health and resilience. The farm provides far more space per fish than do standard fish farms, giving them freedom of *mobility* and creating a much more **distributed** system, which greatly improves their health and well-being and reduces the risk of disease and pollution. And because the farm doesn't feed its fish but allows them to feed on their ecosystem, as they would in the wild, it maintains their **autonomy**.

The farm pumps its water in from the nearby river and back out to it further downstream. As the water passes through the farm it is cleaned and purified by the aquatic ecosystem so that it leaves the farm *cleaner* than when it arrived. The fish are caught and sold only in response to specific demand from restaurants, fishmongers, and other customers, creating a **continuity** of extremely fresh supply in small batches, reducing waste, and maintaining exceptionally high quality. In terms of **shared success**, it is a farm that does not shoot, poison, or otherwise deter its predators—in this case flamingos, who consume up to 20% of the shrimp that also feed the fish and that the farm sells as one of its products—but instead measures the success of the farm by the well-being of those predators. The farm's leader, biologist Miguel Medialdea, takes a **connected** and **shared** view, claiming, "I'm not an expert in fish; I'm an expert in relationships." He doesn't view the 20% of the shrimp eaten by flamingos as lost revenue. He says, "We farm extensively, not intensively. This is an ecological network. The flamingos eat the shrimp. The shrimp eat the phytoplankton. The pinker the belly, the better the system."

It is a farm whose activities do not pollute or impoverish the environment but actually purify and enrich it. As such, it has also become a bird and wildlife sanctuary—home to over 250 species of birds, 50 of which are recorded as being endangered elsewhere—and it provides direct income to about 100 people from the neighboring villages. It is a remarkable and successful experiment in the Boundless approach to resource management. And, according to Chef Barber, the fish tastes absolutely delicious!

We will revisit regenerative agriculture and aquaculture in Chapters 5 and 9, because they represent such an important and broadly applicable example of the Boundless mindset.

Tesla and the Transformation of the Automobile

The second case study is in the automotive industry, a newcomer compared to the 10,000 years of agriculture, but nevertheless one of our most mature industries in terms of market penetration and technological performance. That is why the current Boundless revolution—in electrification and digitalization—is so remarkable and so likely to have huge implications on multiple sectors within just a few years from now.

In 2021 Tesla became the first car company to reach (however briefly) a trillion-dollar market capitalization (Sankaran, 2021). And although its current valuation at the time of writing (February 2023) hovers at about 60% of its all-time high, many market analysts and investors see it going a great deal higher within the next few years (e.g., Root, 2022).

What separates Tesla from its competitors is its combination of electronics, autonomous hardware and software, AI-powered applications, and autonomous driving data. Autonomous cars are far more **connected** to the outside world than are traditional models. To function effectively and safely, autonomous cars have to sense the other cars and conditions around them and know about changing conditions along the way (e.g., a crash that has slowed traffic on that particular road). They also have to be connected to their maker to ensure it receives any necessary upgrades. In the future we can expect cars to be more connected still, to charging stations between trips, to garages—or perhaps to mechanobots—when they self-diagnose problems, and to people who want them for individual journeys as robotaxis or autonomous car shares.

An essential part of the autonomous car is its ability to perceive and make sense of all the data that comes in from the outside world via its sensors or connection points. All this data is **integrated** to provide a 360-degree view of the immediate environment and to enable the artificial intelligence onboard to make effective decisions.

As a fleet, the individual autonomous cars will be integrated with one another. And thanks to their individual and collective intelligence, as well as the integrated intelligence of a fleet-orchestration function, it will be possible to ensure that their geographic **distribution** is optimized to reduce wait times for any individual customer and to reduce the size of the fleet—and hence the energy consumed—that is required to meet the overall demand.

In the current schema, the "most" **autonomous** cars (Level 5) will be able to complete a journey end to end without human intervention. This requires a high degree of intelligence to sense, perceive, decide, and act on all data along the way. But true autonomy goes far beyond even that ability of self-nourishment, self-diagnosis, self-healing, self-improvement, and even some level of self-determination; the car of the future might have the ability to determine whether it's safe or even "wise" to undertake a requested journey.

In the future, the **mobility** of the autonomous car will be enhanced, especially in heavy traffic, because autonomous cars are anticipated to flow more smoothly together without individual human driver behaviors and styles clogging things up. And autonomous cars' **shared success** will come from the fact that they will open up travel and transport to those currently regarded as unfit to drive, such as the elderly, the young, and the disabled. It will also transform the experience for all humans, who will be free to engage in leisure or business activities as travelers rather than as machine operators. And it will be *much* safer for all who travel on or alongside roads (like pedestrians and cyclists), because the vast majority of all car crashes are caused by human behaviors, including fatigue, intoxication, aggression, and distraction (Bieber, 2023). This should also lead to less damage to the cars themselves. Electrification throughout will enhance the ability of the cars to take in information and make decisions—and will of course also provide priceless environmental benefit through reduced consumption of fossil fuels and emission of carbon monoxide. Overall, the transformation from traditional to autonomous driving will augur improvements in relationships, access, and safety for all.

★ ★ ★

In conclusion, Boundless organizations are guided by the principle of shared success. They create win-win, win-win-win, and even win-win-win-win-win(!) situations, and they all share most or all of the six principles of connection, distribution, integration, autonomy, mobility, and continuity. This is a powerful finding. Business models for designing customer experiences, products, and services that use these principles can increase the chances of companies delivering multithreaded successes like the ones described here—thus increasing the chances of becoming Boundless. In the chapters ahead we will focus on each principle in turn.

3 | Connection

Relationships | Ecosystems | Sensing

"When we try to pick out anything by itself, we find it hitched to everything else in the Universe."

—*John Muir (1911)*

Unlike their silo counterparts, which favor isolation and demarcation, Boundless entities are connected to the outside world, to their customers, and to the markets or ecosystems of which they are a part. They sense what's happening in their environment and with all members and parts of it, and they are able to respond effectively to those signals and changes.

Types of Connections

To follow we elaborate on some of these types of connections.

Natural Connections

Among us humans, connection and interaction with the world around us is established via the sensory organs: the eyes, ears, nose, mouth, and skin. (We're not able to speak about other potential ways of sensing, such as proprioception or energy transmission.) Other animals have more or less advanced forms of the same senses. Some dolphins, whales, and bats navigate and track prey using echolocation. Sharks also sense changes in their surroundings via electroreception, taking advantage of the ability of salt in the water to conduct electric currents emanating from the muscular movement of fish. And many birds, as well as honeybees, ants, and termites, are able to navigate via magnetoreception, connecting to the world in a way we still don't truly understand.

In trees, connections are made via leaves and the bark above ground and via roots and mycorrhizal fungal networks (which are not parts of the tree themselves) underground. The recent (by humans at least) discovery of this so-called wood wide web has shed light on the ability of trees—or even of different species—to communicate and share resources with one another, increasing their own success as well as the overall success of the forest of which they are a part (Wohlleben, 2016).

The point perhaps is this: the more we learn about our own species, other animals, and even plants, and the more we learn about living systems, the more connected with each other and with the world about them we find them to be.

Of killer whales Charles Foster (2019) writes, "[T]heir whole lives are relational. The individuals in a community may have radically different personalities, but the boundaries between them are ecstatically blurred. Individuals bleed into one another."

Extended and Enhanced Connections

We humans have always used technologies to connect us, physically as well as virtually. Houses are physically connected to their surroundings—not only by the driveway and the garden path but also by the sewer system, the electrical grid, the natural gas network, the phone network (in the case of the traditional home phone system), the TV network, and the internet.

The house is also connected by intermittent or periodic systems, most importantly by weekly garbage disposal, mail delivery, and increasingly by e-commerce package delivery. The ice cream van may also serve to connect the home to the community in the summer months.

Technology has enabled us not only to connect with the world but also to extend ourselves into it and to have influence beyond the limits of our physical bodies. For instance, every single form of human communication, beyond talking face-to-face or calling/shouting/whistling from a distance, is mediated in some way by technology. From smoke signals and hillside fires to clay tablets and knotted strings, from telegram and morse code to Facebook and Snapchat, all communication is technology enabled. And communication extends our selves, our thoughts and desires, out into the minds of others.

The American Association for the Advancement of Science draws attention to the role of technology in extending, or providing, capabilities to those that have lost them or were born without them: "Tools provide us with delicate control and prodigious strength and speed. For example, telescopes, cameras, infrared sensors, microphones, and other instruments extend our visual, auditory, and tactile senses and increase their sensitivity. Prosthetic devices and chemical and surgical intervention enable people with physical disabilities to function more effectively in their environment" (Science for All Americans Online, 1990).

Marshall McLuhan (1964) developed the theme in his analysis of electronic media, noting that more recent technologies extend not just our physical capabilities but also our sensory and cognitive ones: "During the mechanical ages we had extended our bodies in space. Today, after more than a century of electronic technology, we have extended our central nervous system itself in a global embrace, abolishing time and space as far as our planet is concerned" (p. 19).

And now, we are in the early years of the autonomous era, when sensory devices rather than organs are enabling things—machines, tools, products, built systems—to connect to one another and to carry out work without direct human intervention. As we discussed in an earlier post, the connection of the autonomous car is achieved by sensors, in particular camera, radar, light detection and ranging, GPS, and inertial measurement unit. All of these provide a real time moving picture of the car's immediate road and roadside environment including other vehicles, traffic lights and signals, road markings, pedestrians, cyclists, vehicle attachments (like bikes on bike racks), and all other components of the immediate surroundings. Connection is also achieved via the internet to the vehicle's manufacturer or other sources to access software downloads to enhance or modify the vehicle's performance, and we can expect greater connection over time between the vehicle and others nearest it, potentially enabling collective intelligence and decision-making (e.g., herding or flocking behaviors) that will increase the efficiency of the traffic on the road as a whole.

Business Connections

Living systems and autonomous systems alike are dependent on connections with the world around them to survive and thrive. This is
no less true for business systems. So what are the eyes and ears of a
company? What is its skin? Any organization must be able to sense
all customer touchpoints, whether those are in person, by phone,
email, website and so on, and whether they are informational, transactional, or assistance related. Without effective e-commerce, points
of sale, helpdesks, and other systems and processes to enable those
touchpoints, the company may simply be blind or deaf to their customer needs. For a company to remain successful it must become
increasingly connected, and its connections must become increasingly sensitive.

Other direct touch points include those with supply, channel,
and/or distribution partners with whom the company does business,
followed by investors and other stakeholders. Maintaining direct links
with schools and other parts of the community enables them to
understand the needs and skills of the future workforce and other key
stakeholders.

Second, the organization must be aware of changes to the environment, broadly the market, and economic conditions in which
they operate, including the actions of competitors, emergent technologies, new regulations, and any other factors that change the
nature of the ecosystem. Maintaining an active investment capability
is one way that companies can keep current on new technological
developments.

The extent to which a company can sense its customers, its ecosystem, and the environment more broadly will dictate the extent to
which it will be able to model the five other Boundless principles and
thus operate successfully. And this is not a one-time activity; it's continuous. As new technologies continue to emerge and evolve,

customers and all other stakeholders will have new superpowers—new ways of connecting—and they will expect their providers to be able to respond.

In this chapter, then, we focus on relationships, ecosystems, and the power of sense.

Relationships

Business success in this new age, one that is sometimes called the fourth industrial revolution, comes from getting the human parts of the equation right. Although digital technologies are often held up as the stars of the show in the business world, in reality it's people that need to take center stage, with technologies playing vital supporting roles. Managing relationships with customers in this era is more important than ever before, but the key to sustained growth and success for companies comes from transforming those relationships, and not only with their customers but also with their employees, partners, and communities.

All Relationships Are Changing

We are in the early days of this revolution, an era that builds on the digital computing capabilities developed during the last half of the 20th century: embedding intelligence into previously dumb things, discovering and developing powerful new materials, revolutionizing manufacturing practices and capabilities, and expanding our understanding of the human genome and creating new possibilities for extending our health and our lives.

One of the most significant impacts of these advances is to amplify and accelerate the changes in our relationships that the previous revolutions had already put in place. Our research tells us that these relationships are all changing, all at once, as established ones seem to be failing us or are no longer relevant, and we're looking for new models to replace them. And the changes are pervasive throughout every area of our lives, in our home and family lives, our social and cultural lives, our roles as producers-providers and consumers, and even in our interactions with things and places.

Home and Family   Where and how and with whom we live is changing dramatically. Prior to the first and second industrial revolutions, the eras of steam and of electricity, a large majority of all people across the world lived in rural communities. The advances in technology drew people together in larger towns and cities as production at scale became possible for the first time. But it was not until as recently as 2007 that more than 50% of the world's population lived in an urban setting. In 1950 New York was the only city in the world to have 10 million inhabitants, the definition of a megacity. By 1985 there were nine megacities across the world and now, in 2023, there are 38 of them, mostly in Asia (CIOB, 2023).

Meanwhile, our family units are also changing. The 2010 US Census (US Census Bureau, 2023) is the first time in which "traditional" families headed by a married heterosexual couple represent less than half of all households. The number of people per household has also shrunk by nearly a whole person since 1960, and the number of single-person households has more than doubled in the same time, now representing nearly 28% of all households.

Society and Culture   Our relationships with cultural and social leaders are changing. We are losing our trust in "establishment" figures in all walks of life as sporting heroes are uncovered as cheats; religious, political, and entertainment leaders are found lying to us or are denounced as sex offenders; and experts of various kinds are delegitimized by false claims, mistakes, and ambiguity in theory and prediction. And instead we are turning toward non-establishment individuals as our influencers and leaders. This is a world, for instance, in which a six-year-old boy can make $11 million from his online reviews of toys.

Meanwhile, as individuals, we now have technologies that transform our own capabilities and enable us to develop relationships with others who are more aligned with our needs. We are now tooled, informed, skilled, connected, and autonomous. We are finding communities of interest online, with no concern for physical distance between us. And when it suits us we share freely with one another our knowledge, practical (e.g., DIY videos on YouTube) and reference (e.g., Wikipedia), as well as our talents and interests (e.g., TikTok, Instagram), creating remarkable accomplishments that have no close precedent in our history.

Production and Consumption Our relationships with work and our employers are changing, too, although not necessarily in the ways we might have heard. The percentage of the employable population that is in full-time employment has, for instance, remained more or less unchanged for decades, with employment tenures for the "average" worker as well as the CEO remaining remarkably constant and even increasing. Even the much touted gig economy, if defined in terms of people who report having multiple jobs, has actually been shrinking since the mid-1990s.

And yet what is changing is the kind of jobs we are doing and are likely to be doing. Looking back, in 1870 nearly half the US population worked in agriculture. Now less than 2% do. And looking forward it is widely believed that the most sought-after jobs in the next decade, and likely the most highly paid ones, do not yet even exist. Meanwhile, some of today's most common jobs, including truck driving, accounting, and call center support are threatened with extinction as a result of emerging technologies such as autonomous vehicles, the blockchain, and interactive voice response.

Meanwhile our habits and behaviors as consumers are changing dramatically. We are no longer bound to passive models of consumption. In 2016 and 2017 many of the nation's 10- to 14-year-old girls were smitten by an unlikely passion: slime. Now, fads are not in themselves exceptional, but this time around the girls weren't just buying a commercial product to play with. This time they were buying raw materials, innovating and designing new versions of the stretchy, slimy stuff, making DIY videos and posting them on YouTube, giving live demonstrations via Instagram Live Video, and even packaging and selling their products on Etsy. They have transcended all traditional definitions of the "consumer" and will likely pose interesting challenges and opportunities for employers and producers alike in a decade or so when they are young adult women with quite different definitions, experiences, and expectations of work and play. We'll look more deeply at the slime phenomenon in Chapter 6.

Things and Places   It's not just our relationships with each other, with people, that are changing. Our relationships with things and places are evolving, too.

The TV is still our dominant form of screen-based entertainment but mobile platforms are fast catching up. The first smartphone, the iPhone, was launched in 2007 and the growth has been extraordinary, with an estimated more than 5 billion people, or nearly two-thirds of the earth's population, all now using a smartphone. And their profound influence on us is clear for us all to see. But they're just one flavor of the total number of mobile devices worldwide, which has now surpassed 15 billion. They have outnumbered us since 2014 or so and are continuing to increase in number much much faster than we are.

And just over the horizon, but not by much, is the rise of the autonomous car. Americans have a special relationship with their cars, a relationship that has deeply influenced the design of cities and sub-urbs and enabled the growth of companies like Walmart. This relationship is about to change dramatically as our cars become able to alert the driver to danger, respond to collisions, self-park, auto-brake, auto-course correct, and all too soon, drive itself, our first hypermobile robot. The automobile is actually beginning to live up to its name and when it does the US will be transformed once more.

Successful Companies Adapt Accordingly

This all creates major uncertainty, instability, and volatility, but also the promise of new paradigms. The challenge for our companies is how to keep up with it all.

For companies to be successful in this new era, it's more important than ever before that they tap into these paradigm shifts and manage their relationships with their customers. But this is now just table stakes, and it's no longer enough to ensure differentiated and sustained success. Our research tells us that the most successful organizations in this era are achieving their success by *transforming* their relationships. Transforming them into what? You may ask? Well, how about love affairs?

One of our favorite companies is Wegmans. It's a US regional supermarket chain with 109 stores mostly in the Northeast and mid-Atlantic states. It is one of the largest private companies in the US with approximately 52,000 employees and annual sales in 2021 of $11.2 billion. It regularly shows up in "best-of" lists, and is currently (2023) ranked number 3 on *Fortune* magazine's list of the 100 Best Companies to Work For. It has appeared on that list every year since it began in 1998, and in 2005, ranked number 1. It is a company with strong values centered on their people, customers, and communities. But what we love most about Wegmans is that it has transformed their everyday customers into diehard fanatics, otherwise known as

Wegmaniacs, who (with their own Twitter group naturally, #wegmania) have been known to travel hundreds of miles to new store openings. On Sunday, September 24, 2017, Wegmans opened a store in Montvale, New Jersey. Approximately 20,000 people showed up to the opening day, about two and a half times the number of people who actually live in Montvale. And that wasn't even a record. The first store to open in New Jersey had 24,000 visitors on opening day. And this is not exactly an Apple or a Goyard selling limited quantities of high-demand, high-end items. This is a supermarket selling groceries.

And then there's the love letters. Wegmans receives thousands of them every year from customers who beg the company to open a store near them or who simply want to thank them. And for its part, the company keeps a record of them and uses them as a key performance indicator. It's a small thing perhaps but it's a human thing and it lets the customers know that Wegmans loves them right back.

Boundless companies seek to transform their relationships not only with their customers but also with their employees, partners, communities, and all other stakeholders. This is the Boundless mindset. It's important to remember that these are not only times of great disruption and crisis but also opportunities for positive change with relationships at the center of transformation. To do this they can start by doing the following:

First, focus on earning **customer trust**. Trust is the cornerstone of successful relationships. Customers are becoming more demanding of the people and organizations with whom they do business. COVID-19 is only making this reality more profound. But when they trust them and are fully engaged, they buy 90% more frequently, spend 60% more, and are 5 times more likely to indicate exclusive loyalty (Bansal, 2015). So there's a direct line from trust to loyalty to reduced costs and increased revenues. All of which suggests that trust should be a top priority for CEOs and a core part of any organization's strategy for growth. But being a strategy is not enough. To be authentic, trust needs to be a core value, one that all employees, not just the CEO, model and strive after in all their activities and behaviors.

Second, on **living their values and purpose**. Eighty percent of customers and employees believe businesses have a responsibility to make a positive impact on society and are more likely to want to be associated with them than those that are purely profit driven. If there was ever a time to demonstrate purpose, this is it. Remember, one-third of customers don't believe businesses will do the right thing, 36% feel that social initiatives are superficial, and 42% feel that businesses are taking self-interested actions. It should then serve as no surprise that purpose-driven organizations outperform the S&P 500 by a factor of 10 according to Bain & Company (Reichheld et al., 2021).

Third, on **building ecosystems**, which entails building connections not only with their customers but also with all their business partners, employees, other stakeholders, and their communities (see the next section, "Business Ecosystems"). Business ecosystems create explosive growth in this era. Seven of the top 12 largest companies by market capitalization— Alibaba, Alphabet (Google), Amazon, Apple, Facebook, Microsoft, and Tencent—are ecosystem players (McKinsey, 2018).

This reframing of digital transformation on relationships is more inclusive and purposeful because it embraces all corporate functions and puts humans and human outcomes first. Relationships are the responsibility of everyone in the organization and are also the principal means by which organizational culture and business ecosystems get built. COVID-19 is only magnifying the need and opportunity. By shifting the focus of transformation away from entities such as business, technology, and even individual people, and instead focusing on the connections between them, it avoids the implication that the entities are somehow faulty or to blame for the current state and that they therefore need to be fixed or changed.

Everyone agrees that companies need to improve the ways they do business, and the stakes have never been higher. If they're going to succeed they have to adapt to the evolving digital age and to a world completely reset by the coronavirus. But the stars in any contemporary business transformation are the people, and what drives the action is not the people themselves but the relationships between them.

In Chapter 10 we will offer up some thoughts on what makes a successful relationship and how to design for one.

Business Ecosystems

Boundless success in the digital era will come from the connected and collaborative efforts of business ecosystems more than from the controlled efforts of individual companies. Managers don't need to acquire new capabilities or resources or technologies to start ecosystem building, but they do need to adopt an ecosystem mindset first to make their efforts authentic and their success more likely.

The most evolved digital business ecosystem is probably that of Alibaba.

Alibaba: the Digital Ecosystem   Founded by Jack Ma, Alibaba is a Chinese e-commerce giant. It started off life in 1999 as a business-to-business online marketplace (alibaba.com) and quickly grew in size and profitability, leading to the launch of a consumer-to-consumer platform in 2004 (taobao.com) and a business-to-consumer platform in 2008 (tmall.com). The company is now one of the biggest multinational technology companies in the world and has ventured into many other fields beyond its core platforms—including financial services, in which it is now the world's fourth largest fintech player by market valuation, behind only Visa, Mastercard, and Tencent, its Chinese competitor.

Of particular interest here is the way that Alibabas's leaders describe it. In a fascinating article for *Harvard Business Review*, Ming Zeng (2018), Alibaba's former chief strategy officer and current chairman of the Academic Council of the Alibaba Group, tells of a leadership offsite in 2007 where they developed an ecosystem mindset. They agreed that fostering "the development of an open, coordinated, prosperous e-commerce ecosystem" should not be a beneficial by-product of the company's platform but should instead be the company's vision, and that what they needed to focus on and get right as a company was ensuring that their platform(s) provided the resources, or access to resources, that would enable the ecosystem to thrive.

Ecosystem may sound like a buzzword but the reality is that for platform companies their ecosystem is key to their ongoing growth and resilience. A platform's value includes not just the core functionality that is developed by the platform owner itself but all the additional capabilities developed by ecosystem members, and it increases with each additional capability and/or ecosystem member. The ecosystem protects the platform from competition, builds user loyalty toward it, and protects the platform from becoming irrelevant. Meanwhile, the productivity and innovation of the ecosystem grows as its population grows.

For Ming Zeng, this is the future of business, a Boundless company that grows in value as the volume and speed of data flowing across the ecosystem increases. He calls this "smart business" and believes that it takes four main steps to becoming one. Those steps are first to "datafy" every customer transaction in order to make sure new data gets captured. Second to "software" every business activity so that decisions can then be automated. Third to "get data flowing" across and throughout the ecosystem, which requires integration. It is the data that counts. "The more data flows across the network, the smarter the business becomes, and the more value the ecosystem creates." And finally to apply the algorithms to all the data to improve accuracy and speed of decision-making and action taking. In short, according to Ming Zeng: "To become a smart business, your firm must enable as many operating decisions as possible to be made by machines fueled by live data rather than by humans supported by their own data analysis."

As we will see in the section, "The Power of Sense," handing decision-making over to machines may not be the easiest thing for human leaders to do, especially for those who are not digital natives as well as for those who believe that their job as leader is to make the decisions. And, as we have already suggested, following this model leads toward the blurring of boundaries between organization and technology. Any organization and any business ecosystem that follows Ming Zeng's advice of datafying, softwaring, integrating, and algorithmizing (admittedly a very strange combination of neologisms) is more or less indistinguishable from the technology itself. And from a Boundless perspective, the difference between Connection and Integration becomes more and more blurred as an organization becomes ever more closely connected to its ecosystem.

Ecosystems can be physical as well, and although the shared resources may appear very different—for example, water, waste, and by-product rather than data—the principles are extremely similar and the main goal is to create economic value for both or all parties involved in the exchanges and to generate value as well for consumers, communities, and in some cases the environment. Whereas Alibaba is the poster child for digital business ecosystems, the Danish industrial park in Kalundborg is widely regarded as the world's longest standing and most complete example of an industrial ecosystem.

Kalundborg: The World's First Industrial Symbiosis   Kalundborg stands alone in its commitment to industrial symbiosis, the sharing between organizations of by-products as resources, including water, energy, and material, to reduce waste, costs, and environmental pollution. Since its initial experiments in 1972, membership in this industrial ecosystem—or what is now known as Kalundborg Symbiosis (https://www.symbiosis.dk/en/)—has grown to include over 30 by-product exchange agreements among 14 public and private companies in Kalundborg, including some of Denmark's largest organizations, in what it describes as "50 years of circular production." The Symbiosis saves money for its participants, minimizes waste, creates growth in the local community, and benefits the environment.

This ecosystem works as a series of company-to-company exchanges in which one company's waste or by-product becomes another company's raw materials or other resource. These by-products include water, steam, heat, gas, ash, sludge, and others that can be physically transported from one company to another. Each exchange benefits the sending and the receiving company economically. The sender makes money from its ability to sell its by-product resource streams and saves money by eliminating or at least reducing the cost of waste transportation and/or remediation. The receiver saves money by obtaining energy and/or material resources at a competitive price with lower cost of transportation because all the companies in the ecosystem are located in relatively close proximity to one another. The two companies do comprehensive financial analysis of the exchange, including the expected return on investment from pipeline construction as applicable and any other equipment needed to exchange the resources, before signing an agreement between them. This mutual economic benefit is recognized by the Symbiosis as critical to the ongoing success of the entire ecosystem.

The municipality's Asnaes power plant, owned and operated by Ørsted (ranked the world's most sustainable energy company), has long been at the heart of the ecosystem, exchanging multiple resource streams with other members of it. It has provided enough steam to the local Equinor oil refinery to account for up to 40% of its heating needs as well as enough to Novo Nordisk (the world's biggest supplier of insulin) to cover all of its heating and processing needs at a reported savings to them of up to $1 million annually.

Until 2017, Asnaes was coal powered and by-products from its process included fly ash and clinker, which it then sold as material for building roads and making cement. In addition it produced industrial gypsum as a by-product (after treatment), which it sold to Gyproc, a local company that makes wallboards. It charged comparative prices for its gypsum as Gyproc would pay for mined gypsum imported from Spain but at significantly lower freight costs.

Since 2017, however, when Ørsted converted the power plant from being coal fired to wood chip fired in pursuit of its own sustainability goals, it no longer produced industrial gypsum as a by-product and so was no longer able to supply Gyproc with that resource. The Symbiosis is looking for new ways to supply it with local resources to reduce costs and limit the quantity of gypsum that it needs to mine and to transport. In the meantime, the power plant now produces water from burning the wood chips and this new stream is being used by the oil refinery in its process.

All of this points to an ongoing evolution individually and collectively toward greater sustainability over time. Among the members, they generate the following annual environmental benefits: a reduction in CO_2 emission by 586,000 tons, a savings of 4 million cubic meters of water through recycling and reuse, and the recycling of 62,000 tons of residual materials.

The current plans of the Symbiosis (as of late 2022) include a sharing agreement between the municipality of Kalundborg and the neighboring municipality of Holbæk with plans to capture the heat produced by all the companies in the ecosystem and distribute it as district heating, via a heat pump, to all the citizens of both municipalities. It also has longer term plans to extend the Symbiosis beyond industrial processes and companies to biotech.

The park as a whole operates as a continuous-flow system, providing inspiration, example, and analogy for innovative multi-organizational collaborations of all types. With the recent increased interest in business ecosystems and in sustainability, Kalundborg continues to serve as an important inspiration and is looking to become even more connected globally. In 2018 the Symbiosis was awarded the Win-Win Gothenburg Sustainability Award. This award is given each year to people or organizations for their outstanding contributions toward a sustainable future. Previous winners of the award include Kofi Annan and Al Gore.

The Principles of Ecosystems

Companies have, of course, always been part of value chains, with their own supply and channel partners, but they have largely maintained a worldview based on themselves as individual and independent business entities. Going it alone in the digital age, however, is no longer a strategy for success. "If the old world was about keeping things proprietary and closed off, the new world is about engaging with an ecosystem of partners and vendors. This approach can help accelerate access to markets, talent, capabilities, and technologies . . . and help businesses get smart quickly about how to 'do digital'" (McKinsey & Co, 2017).

There are major advantages to building an ecosystem, even for those companies that aren't platform businesses, but building an ecosystem doesn't just happen. It takes planning, patience, and a lot of hard work on the part of a lot of people. In our experience, the most difficult part of building an ecosystem is the very first part: making the shift from the dominant siloed mindset of individual companies toward the new and emerging Boundless mindset of connected ecosystems. Here are five mindset shifts and connective strategies that managers need to understand, make, and assimilate fully as a prerequisite to successful ecosystem building:

Mindset shift 1: From independence to interdependence. Although we have all grown up in a culture that rewards individual achievement, ecosystem companies are achieving unprecedented success by enabling others to be successful. It's easy to forget that the iPhone was originally designed as closed system but was opened up to others via the App Store in 2008, and an explosion of ideas and new apps followed. Within a decade, third-party developers were being paid over $26.5 billion and the App Store has developed into the company's fastest-growing and highest-margin significant business.

Mindset shift 2: From controlling to collaborating. Companies typically drive new product development with their own people, in full control of process, and with complete ownership of emerging concepts. GE Appliances upended this model with Firstbuild, a stand-alone innovation lab with a mix of employees and community members. They design and build innovative home appliances on an open source model, prove initial market demand, and then enter revenue-sharing agreements with any products that GE itself chooses to scale. Founded in 2014, Firstbuild is now an independent entity, but it is backed by the resources and know-how of GE and staffed in part by engineering students from the University of Louisville on whose campus the facility is located.

Mindset shift 3: From protecting to sharing. Organizations the world over vigorously protect their brands, intellectual property and data from outsiders. But some see greater value in sharing. Goldcorp, a Canadian mining company, had spent years unsuccessfully looking for the exact location of gold deposits that their tests had flagged. They published all their geological data on the web with $575,000 in prize money for anyone who could help them find the missing gold. And the quality and value of the responses shocked them, leading to 60 new drilling sites, 8 million ounces of gold, a two- to three-year reduction in exploration and a surge in revenue from $100 million to $9 billion.

Mindset shift 4: From linear to interwoven. Innovation within a typical company, and even within a typical supply chain, is like a relay race. You do your part and then hand off the baton to the next in line and hope that no one drops it. An ecosystem can accelerate time to market by working on product development and other innovation together when possible and in parallel when not. GlaxoSmithKline, for example, is partnering with scientists, researchers, field workers, and relief agencies in order to accelerate the fight against malaria. They have published data on 13,500 compounds in their chemical library and shared them with 160 research groups around the world to inform and assist in parallel efforts.

Mindset shift 5: From company size to membership size. In the ecosystem worldview, growth—in capabilities, resilience, and success—comes from increasing the number of network members, or *nodes*, not from increasing the size of any single member. Comparatively small companies and even individuals can have outsized impact when they can build or connect to a large-enough ecosystem. A six-year-old "influencer" can now build a YouTube community on his toy reviews and make $11 million per year from the companies that would once have sought control but now see the value from being a supporting ecosystem node.

Success in building a vibrant business ecosystem in the digital economy will be the difference between being marginalized and prospering. Shifting existing mindsets is never easy, but it's an essential first step in that process.

The Power of Sense

It is the various different ways of connecting with the world that enable us to sense what's happening in it that is or could be important to us. This is as true of businesses as it is of autonomous vehicles or of us as individuals or of all living things. If we're not connected, we can't sense. And if we can't sense, we're already dead. But if we can sense, we can respond. And we can also anticipate. And increasingly the power to anticipate is more important than ever before. Companies need to use both human and digital capabilities to sense, respond, and anticipate. Sometimes the inputs will be so many, the demands so great, that humans will be simply unable to process them all as accurately and as quickly as their customers and partners demand. Other times the signals may be faint and get lost if not for the one-to-one relationships between the individual sales or service professional and their customer. In the former category, Alibaba's preparedness for the extreme demands of Singles Day stands out, and in the latter we are reminded of a story about Zara, the Spanish fast fashion retailer, and a customer request that encapsulates its approach and shows how it lives up to the expectation of "fast" that defines the industry.

Alibaba and Singles Day

November 11 is Singles Day, chosen for the occasion because of its numerical format 11/11 representing four ones or "single sticks." Singles Day was the invention of a group of Chinese male students in the 1990s, ostensibly as a counterbalance to Valentine's Day and as a way for young single people to celebrate or perhaps bemoan their status and to meet others. It remained largely unknown outside China until 2009 when the e-commerce giant Alibaba (as discussed in the previous section) used it as a pretext for a 24-hour online shopping event. In its first year, Alibaba declared Singles Day gross merchandise value equivalent to approximately $7.8 million. Thanks to truly explosive growth, that figure just a decade later stood at

$38.4 billion, a 5,000 times increase and more than double the combined sales of Black Friday and Cyber Monday in the US that same year! COVID-19 and the global shift online saw that figure double the next year, admittedly with a shopping window expanding to the first 11 days of November rather than just the 11th. Alibaba did not report its 2022 gross merchandise value but declared that it was in line with the previous year's total of roughly $84.5 billion.

The coordination required to pull off this feat, even from just an online transaction processing perspective, is remarkable enough. But what is perhaps even more remarkable is the effort it must take to answer the queries and concerns of tens of millions of customers and to package and deliver all the physical goods sold. As for the former, it was estimated that in 2019 it would have required 85,000 human customer service agents to handle the 300 million plus queries the platform received. Instead Alibaba depended on their customer service chatbot, AliMe, to sense and respond to 97% of them. AliMe is an AI shopping guide and assistant for buyers and sellers and the more customers it responds to the smarter it gets and more able to predict what help they might need and what products they might like. As we saw previously, data in terms of high volumes of live data is what AI uses to learn and improve and increase its value to the human and digital ecosystem over time.

As for the packaging and delivery of physical goods, Alibaba uses AI to anticipate exactly what products will be ordered and in what combinations. This allows Alibaba and its suppliers to box up hundreds of thousands of items ahead of Singles Day and take a huge burden off them on gameday.

Zara and the Pink Scarf Story

Zara is one of our favorite examples of the principle of *continuity* by being a company whose entire business model is based on the principles of designing, producing, shipping, and selling small batches of fashion products and doing so on a continuous basis. In the process it has become the most successful retail fashion company in the world by revenue and has kept that position for at least the last 15 years—since 2008. So we'll come back to it at greater length in Chapter 8, but there is one story, first told by brand strategist Martin Roll that is particularly relevant here:

> [A] lady named Miko walked into a Zara store in Tokyo and asked the store assistant for a pink scarf, but the store did not have any pink scarves. The same happened almost simultaneously for Michelle in Toronto, Elaine in San Francisco, and Giselle in Frankfurt, who all walked into Zara stores and asked for pink scarves. They all left the stores without any scarves. . . .7 days later, more than 2,000 Zara stores globally started selling pink scarves. 500,000 pink scarves were dispatched—to be exact. They sold out in three days. (MartinRoll, 2021)

From a sense and respond perspective there are few better stories anywhere. Individual sales professionals at stores picked up on the individual requests and reported them to the design center in Spain, where it was quickly realized that this was an opportunity. Because of their continuous design, production, and shipping business model they were able to respond, and in 10 days from beginning to end they had sold half a million pink scarves.

Sensing and Inherent Instability

A Boundless company must be able to sense situationally and horizontally. And there will be so many inputs that it will need AI to respond effectively, in the same way that pilots of inherently unstable airplanes need technology to sense, understand, and respond to all the inputs they get on a real-time basis.

The latest generation of fighter aircraft often employ design elements that reduce stability to increase maneuverability and responsiveness. The problem is that these characteristics, which are highly desirable from a combat performance perspective, will typically make control by a pilot difficult or impossible, hence the expression *inherent instability*. To compensate, stability is typically imposed artificially using computers, servos, and sensors as parts of a fly-by-wire control system.

This is what makes these aircraft such a compelling but nonobvious metaphor for today's businesses. You need instability to be Agile, you need AI to help handle (not remove) the instability. **In the past, our companies were designed for stability, for predictability. Now we have to build them for instability, for responsiveness.** Highly responsive businesses will also inevitably be unstable businesses. You can be resistant and stable—which is what we've tried— but you can't be responsive and stable.

The challenge for human leaders is to realize and accept that they can no longer control their company. And worse, they have to realize and accept that they have to make their company even less easy for them to control. This will lead to a real dilemma. As leaders try to make their companies more responsive to change in customer needs and expectations, to market forces, and to continuous technological innovation, the more they will feel that they're losing control. Their natural instinct will be to take back control, but if they do, they will lose the responsiveness they need. There will be a moment of crisis in the transition of control from human leaders to AI when the leaders sense the loss and experience it as a danger to the company, not as an opportunity. And at that moment they will need to fight the urge to take back control and instead push the company beyond the crisis, beyond the turning point. They will need to rip off the bandage and hand decision-making over to the machines, or rather to the software that drives them. This is part of the mindset shift from siloed to Boundless. It simply will not be possible to sense and make sense of and respond to all the data coming at us. Our role will be to be creative and human and to foster the best relationships that we possibly can.

That's why we need to change the metaphors we use for business. We can no longer use metaphors from the immovable built place and should instead use metaphors from mobility: from autonomous cars, rocket ships, planes, and so on. And from circulatory systems—systems that cause things to move—with components like pumps and filters. This will feel strange at first but is a vital step in changing our mindsets.

Once we're comfortable with these new metaphors we can apply the same operating model to business as we apply to these new autonomous and mobile technologies, individually and collectively. This is the sense, frame, decide, act model that we introduce in Chapter 10. Let's simply observe here that, in this model, everything is dependent on sensing.

4 | Distribution

Decentralizing Technologies |
Remote = Local |
Edges > Centers

"*The action most worth watching is not at the center of things, but where edges meet.*"

—*Anne Fadiman (1997, p. vii)*

In a connected world, business can take place wherever is most convenient or local to the customer. The continuous evolution of technologies toward democratization and decentralization requires businesses to apply the same mindset in their relationships and interactions with their customers and their employees.

COVID-19 and the Definition of Normal

When historians in the future look back on the early years of the 21st century we wonder what they will make of the impact of COVID-19 and the year 2020. Will they see it as an event that changed everything? Or as an event of not much significance except for the tragic loss of life? Or perhaps they will see it as an accelerator of change that was already on its way?

Unsurprisingly, we are in the third camp here. Well before 2020 we had been tracking the growth and evolution of an array of technologies (among them e-commerce, content streaming, the Internet of Things (IoT), 3D printing, cloud-based computing, mobile technologies, autonomous vehicles, telemedicine, the blockchain, and the distributed web) that seemed ripe to transform multiple industries and many parts of our lives, some that were already well on the way to doing so. We also saw that the overwhelming tendency of these technologies was, and is, to support decentralization and democratization of various capabilities. Meaning that where those capabilities—including everything from communicating to manufacturing to running a global business—used to be in the hands of, or available to, a relative few, large organizations, they are now increasingly becoming available to smaller ones, as well as to individuals and those in previously underserved areas.

Yet there were whole swathes of our society, whole industries, that had still not grasped their importance. As we saw in Chapter 1, with few exceptions our companies and institutions before 2020 were operating as centers, accumulating and protecting their resources in order to extract maximum value from them. Even today, CEOs cite their top priorities as growth, scale, and profit (e.g., Gartner, 2022). All other company officers would say that their job is to attract and retain whatever resource they're responsible for (i.e., customers, revenues, employees, data, money, etc.). Also, 90% of all our food comes from large, industrial farms (e.g., Foodindustry.com, 2022), and more and more of our global population is still migrating from rural areas to cities (e.g., Boyd, 2019). We are still in peak silo mode.

So we're not blaming business leaders, or farmers, or teachers for the failures of the model in which they work. But we are saying that the model itself is slow by design, that it is resistant to change by design. But because we are all in it, it is very difficult to see. COVID-19 shined a light on it and on its failure. It enabled us to see clearly how the old normal, our pre-COVID life, was organized, how the next normal will likely be organized, and what companies need to do to bridge the gap.

So let's take a quick look back at 2020. And as a disclaimer, we are obviously viewing the pandemic with a very particular lens. What we are interested in is how the imposition of mass self-quarantining to protect ourselves and each other in absence of a vaccine immediately affected our entire lives.

The logic that led us to the self-quarantining and then to the social distancing was obvious enough and goes something like this: COVID-19 is a virus. Viruses usually spread by physical proximity. One person can infect many people at the same time if they're all in a physical group. This means a virus can spread very quickly across a population that likes to form physical groups and where individuals move from group to group. Given these conditions, a particularly nasty virus could devastate the entire population. To avoid that eventuality, given how much we did not know about the virus at the time, but how much we feared, in March 2020 we stopped forming physical groups. As soon as we did, tens of millions of people lost their jobs and the economy collapsed more or less overnight.

To repeat, as soon as we stopped forming in groups, the economy fell apart. And it wasn't just the economy. Despite all the obvious differences in commerce, education, health care, entertainment, travel and hospitality, religion, and other institutions, they were all organized in the exact same way: a commercial, cultural, and social world based on physical grouping, aggregation, massing, or centralization of people—employees, customers, students, patients, worshippers, travelers, fans and spectators, old people, prisoners, and others—into controlled environments where the associated functions (employment, commerce, education, health care, religion, etc.) took place. In a nutshell, our economy and our old normal were built on and were dependent on centralization.

The response to "normal" crises is to set up centers, often located at and repurposing other centers such as community centers and school gyms: relief centers, advice centers, emergency response centers, places where experts come together, valuable resources are accumulated and victims relocated. But in the case of the coronavirus the exact opposite happened. Centers were closed down everywhere—including offices, schools, stadiums and arenas, theaters, churches, restaurants, and bars—to discourage people from congregating. The advice we were all given, from health professionals, politicians, and our employers, was "stay at home." Don't travel, don't congregate, don't go to the hospital unless you develop symptoms (and even then consider whether you should go); stay at home.

We had to start rewiring our brains to prioritize distribution over centralization and the home over institutions. In this crisis it was not the expert, not the center, that counted. It was the individual citizen, making or keeping their own home a safe space for themselves and their family and practicing this new art of social distancing. What that really meant was disconnecting physically from those centers while maintaining digital connections with our loved ones, our friends, and our communities, and learning from each other via digital and social networks what we should do next. Our strength in 2020 was in our distribution, not in our masses.

This is becoming Boundless. But of course not entirely Boundless, because we also suffered forced isolation and immobility. In the last few years before COVID-19 the health risks of immobility or physical inactivity were becoming more evident, and sitting had become known as "the new smoking." Social isolation became something far too many people experienced in 2020, and studies (e.g., Centers for Disease Control and Prevention, 2021) have shown loneliness can be just as dangerous as inactivity, smoking, and obesity. Isolation and immobility are silo principles (see Chapter 1 on the principles associated with resource control) and more commonly associated with the lives of prisoners, not those of free citizens, and show that our response to COVID-19 was clearly a mix between Boundless and siloed states.

The months that followed the shutdown felt like an extended state of emergency, by just about all measures an abnormal or exceptional set of circumstances. No one wanted to believe that it would become the way we would need to run the economy or live our family and social lives long term and we all hoped that it would give way, sooner or later to a "new normal," whatever that might mean. The negative impact of this limbo or pause between normals on us individually and collectively was huge. Quite apart from the terrible loss of life and livelihood, we witnessed a string of business failures and bankruptcies. We saw disadvantaged communities hit the hardest, and we all experienced firsthand the emotional and psychological effects of isolation and immobilization. And yet there were notable business successes and other positive outcomes as well:

- The phenomenal response by frontline workers
- The extraordinary resilience of individuals, families, and communities
- The explosion in individual creativity and learning
- The noticeable improvement in air quality
- The "return" of birds and other wildlife
- The rapid adoption of remote communications tools for business and personal use
- The acceleration of e-commerce, spearheaded by Amazon, which according to a McKinsey study achieved a 10-year growth in three months
- The accompanying rise in home delivery services
- The long-awaited emergence of telemedicine
- The success of the individual fitness and well-being retail sector
- The success of the home improvement retail sector

The big learning here was that it is possible to be successful without being centralized (again, after solving for isolation and immobilization). And, in fact, it seemed that it might be possible not only for companies to be successful but also for individuals and even for the environment at the same time. In other words, centralization is a choice, not an inevitability or necessity, and there is an emerging alternative that may be more resilient in the face of a systemic threat. In fact we believe that the path to success will increasingly lead away from the centralized model of old and toward the model we have seen emerge most clearly ever since the beginning of the pandemic. This is the model of increasing numbers of employees choosing to work from the home offices they've already equipped, of increasing numbers of consumers and business customers continuing to choose e-commerce, of increasing numbers and types of services (including medical) being delivered virtually, of increasing numbers and types of different education and learning models emerging beyond the physical school, and of increasing volumes and types of goods, perhaps including vaccines, being delivered to people's homes by distributed fleets of autonomous vehicles. All of these things reduce friction and empower connected individuals, providing increasing autonomy while creating a world of new opportunities for companies.

Decentralizing Technologies

This all takes digital technologies to enable and support it, many of which were already very well established before 2020, some of which were taking hold, and other parts of which are still in development. But 2020 will be seen as the year that changed the rate at which all these technologies were adopted. Going forward we will see greater pilot programs and accelerated adoption of autonomous delivery vehicles, digital payments, contactless payment technology, voice and video conferencing, voice-enabled mobile business applications, AI-powered CRM platforms, sensors and wearable health-monitoring technology with greater IoT technologies aimed at automated and autonomous serviceability.

The autonomous vehicle, although in its early stages, is likely to become the most important technology of its time, creating a continuous, mobile, connected distribution system for anything physical, not just people, from any source to any destination, particularly to and from the home. In times of crisis and "normality" alike, we can look to fleets of autonomous vehicles circulating continuously to deliver supplies to our homes, further reducing our dependence on food centers and the lines at checkouts that promote rather than avoid proximity and interaction. These vehicles will not be just cars and trucks but also drones and other purpose-built delivery robots.

And the supplies they will deliver will include not only food but also any other products and raw materials, medicines and drugs, and will do so frequently, quietly, and energy efficiently.

We can likely expect similar, automated distribution solutions for testing, diagnosing, and potentially inoculating or treating people, giving us unprecedented autonomy and even enabling us with the assistance of telemedicine and/or medical AI to self-diagnose and self-treat.

The IoT, and in particular the advent of distributed, additive manufacturing (3D printers and other smart, connected machines), may further challenge the model of centralized, scaled production and enable smaller, more rural or remote communities to build and maintain the things they need locally. Rural regeneration is not reflected by the continuing increase in urban populations across the world but it is hinted at, and enabled by, all these new technologies. With investors such as Steve Case (2022) and his "Rise of the Rest" initiative aiming to reach more of the country's entrepreneurs than those on either coast, we believe that small towns across the country are set for a new, more vital episode in their histories.

We also see how these decentralizing technologies enable different types of relations between providers and consumers. Now, obviously older networks such as TV or radio or the power grid distribute resources to people in their homes and the telephone system enables individuals to make peer-to-peer connections, but more modern networks will enable new levels of interaction between provider and consumer, like teleconsults in health care, as well as enabling many-to-many communications and value flows. Technologies such as solar power enable consumers to feed back surplus energy to the grid, and we can expect the IoT to further accelerate and amplify the flow of information across our networks.

In conclusion, we think that the coronavirus may just accelerate the acceptance and adoption of the Boundless paradigm over business as usual. Our only effective response to the crisis is a digital-first, democratic, distributed one, and we know that many of the technologies that are most likely to disrupt current models are technologies that enable or support distribution.

Remote = Local

But 2020 was not just about technology, of course. Companies of all sizes were understandably desperate to get back to work. The prevailing blueprint for doing so at that time seemed to be one of adapting pre-COVID norms in the short term to account for the virus, using social distancing, masks, staff shifts, or schedules, and so on, on the assumption that a widely available vaccine would sooner or later herald and enable a full return to those norms. But we asked ourselves if the next normal could really just be the old normal plus protection? And even if it were possible to do so, should companies really aim to return to the status quo? Even then we thought not. We believed that the virus and our reaction to it accelerated an emerging shift in our conventional ways of doing things. Companies that returned to the old ways without understanding that shift would be likely to fail.

And so we come to where we are now, early 2023. We have vaccines and boosters—and mask wearing, at least in the US, seems to be dwindling. Many commercial flights seem to be nearly or completely full and the flight attendants ask us to respect our fellow passengers' decisions with regard to those masks. Everything is open. So what comes next? What is or could be the next normal? Does the idea of a "normal" state even mean anything anymore? Obviously we don't know yet. But based on what we learned about life before and during the pandemic, and based on what we believe about the arc of technological evolution and the relative responsiveness to change between silo and Boundless organizations, here's what we think is likely to happen.

The leaders in most companies will instinctively aspire and plan to return to work and resume life as they remembered it. We are seeing this already where leaders are asking their employees to come back into the office. We recognize that some of these leaders are concerned about productivity levels. We think that still others are concerned about their own place and role in such a decentralized world. And there may be still others who question what a company "is" if there is no center, no workplace full of employees in single-occupancy cubicles stationed outside the doors of their managers' office.

Boundless organizations, by contrast, recognize that the continued evolution of decentralizing technologies will create new opportunities for them to serve not only their existing customers and communities but also extend their reach into new, previously hard to serve ones. They will also be able to provide their employees with more choice of how and where to live and work. Companies have for years been moving toward remote workers and distributed teams, but we all know how fragile most video conferencing, document sharing, and other collaborative technologies have been. This may be the moment at which entrepreneurs see the opportunities here for far more compelling remote/distributed experiences that will finally tip the scale to majority remote workforces, reducing real estate costs, emptying out downtowns of daily commuters, and asking the question of where a company's identity might reside if not at HQ.

Boundless organizations question and even reverse the traditional relationship between HQ and "remote" workers. In a connected, networked world it's the HQ that is remote and the remote worker who is local, local to their community and potentially to their customers, that is. The HQ itself should no longer be thought of as a center but instead as a pump, ensuring that all its resources are continuously replenished and refreshed so they can continue to be effective locally. They meet and serve their customers where they are and enable them to maintain their own flow.

This will not be experienced in the same way across all industries, of course. Manufacturing and agriculture for instance are still predominantly hands-on industries and will require employees to come on-site to do their work. However, we expect that the continued innovations in additive manufacturing will create opportunities for much smaller facilities and local businesses to support smaller and more remote communities. As far as agriculture goes, it is well recognized that the regenerative revolution is about replicability, not about scale, with smaller farms providing local communities with employment opportunities as well as with good food. But in broad strokes, we believe that the world of "remote" working is here to stay, and our firms need to fully assimilate what this means for them.

Admittedly, working from home (WFH) has long been a thing among independents, contractors, and the otherwise self-employed, and increasingly among the more digitally connected companies, though not without the occasional fits and starts, like Yahoo!'s famous recall back to the office in 2013 (e.g., Miller & Rampell, 2013). But COVID-19 and the "stay-at-home/safer-at-home" orders have almost certainly accelerated the trend. The vast majority of us are excited to get out of the house, of course, and go about our daily business, becoming free of the shackles of isolation and immobility that those orders imposed on us. But WFH is poised to become much more widespread and perhaps even the norm for some businesses and industries. As we start to move toward this new model of work, however, there are two important things for leaders to consider:

The identity imperative. There is a risk that companies will simply reimagine home as a remote cubicle and forget that the office is more than just real estate. For many people, the physical workplace is where corporate culture and identity exist, where the idea of "company" is made real in the world. Without the logo on the door or at reception, without the security badge, without all the other signage and branded materials, without a space that equates belonging (and reinforces status) with access rights and privileges, identity has to be found in new ways. We believe that purpose and principles or values will become even more important than before to provide that sense of cultural identity and belonging—ideals shared and practiced by all—in the absence of physical collocation. In a 2020 "fireside chat" with Salesforce's CEO Marc Benioff, Kevin Johnson, the CEO of Starbucks, described how doubling down on principles during the pandemic guided their decision-making despite the surrounding uncertainties, and how those principles enabled him to delegate decisions and actions to enable local responsiveness globally. The principles reminded every single Starbucks partner around the world "who" the company is—its DNA, its identity—and therefore what their appropriate action should be in any situation. We will discuss the importance of shared purpose and values in Chapter 5.

Decentralization, not substitution. There is also a risk that the home-based quarantining we have all been living through will harden the concept of home as an extension of the office rather than simply decouple the concepts of work and office. WFH should enable the employee to avoid the wasted time, cost, and discomfort of the commute into the city and enable them instead to do their work wherever (and possibly whenever) feels most conducive to getting it done. This may mean moving to different places over the course of the day. WFH should give the employee their autonomy, not extend the company's authority into their private space. It should also give the company the opportunity to discontinue the use of the word *remote*. Remote is always used to describe distance from HQ when what we really need is a way to describe closeness to the customer. As it happens, remote workers are nearly always closest to the customer while HQ is furthest away, the most remote from them.

For these reasons, we should rebrand WFH as "working from here." It frames the work experience from the user's (employee's) perspective, enabling them to imagine any place as a possible place from which to conduct business, whether that's the office or an officing alternative like WeWork, home itself, a third place like Starbucks, the car (once fully autonomous, of course), a plane, a hotel room or bar, or even the customer's location! It also recognizes that more and more business is being done on mobile devices and that it no longer needs to be place based. Quite simply, wherever I am right now, even if that's in VR, could be a place from where I can work. In other words, here. Working from here.

Edges > Centers

Likewise, customers live and increasingly work outside of centers and expect to be served where they are. As part of the move toward decentralization, leaders need to start using new words, reimagining their own centers, that reflect the paradigm shift.

In the days before the internet became mainstream, companies could think of themselves as centers, because they really were the holders of power and resources, the centers of attraction and attention. Customers had little more than corporate advertising to inform them and influence their purchasing decisions. They were limited, relatively speaking, to mass, passive consumption. Digital technologies were too expensive, too specialized, and too limited for home use by anyone other than enthusiasts. Companies ruled the roost and had little incentive to engage with consumers, focusing instead on operational excellence, making sure their insides were working, that their center was strong. Their goal was profit and growth.

But the problem is that, as consumers, we're not living in that old world any more. We're living in a new world where we're all connected and we have masses of information and we can block ads and instead read user reviews or watch the latest unboxing video. We are more autonomous, more situationally aware, more influential, and more empowered. We can run our own businesses with worldwide reach and no infrastructure. The corporation is no longer all powerful. It now often seems bloated and slow, struggling to keep up despite all those cost reductions.

That's not to say that customers don't want their companies to be connected to them. They do, and in fact they'll quickly choose another provider if you're not. And when they do want to buy something or be served or have their questions answered, they want individual, personal attention wherever they are, and they don't want to wait. But until then they want you to put yourselves at their edge, on their periphery, and wait quietly until they need you.

In the connected world the company's internal hierarchy is irrelevant. Everything that is actually important to our business success and growth, namely, our customers, our partners, and our communities, is on the outside. So it's time for us to create and use new metaphors. We need to learn how to be part of networks that we do not control or own. We need to spend less time thinking like companies and more time like our customers. Which means we need to spend more time focused on the edges, on the outside. After all, as customers, as individuals, as families and as communities, we're all already there.

An interesting side note is that Jack Welch was the hero of those pre-internet days and was known for his unwavering focus on profit and growth. And yet he also was the first to coin the term "the Boundaryless Organization." Boundless and the Boundaryless Organization actually have much in common, most obviously a desire to break down internal and external silos in order to increase effectiveness. But whereas the Boundaryless Organization is primarily focused on the design of the organization itself, Boundless focuses equally on the design of experiences, solutions, business processes, and operating models. We use the same set of seven design principles to apply across these different domains. Boundless is also more focused on the ever-evolving world of technology and the emerging opportunities that it offers for connection, distribution, and integration across organizations, ecosystems, and communities. And finally the Boundless mindset is one that recognizes the possibility of designing for shared success, for win-win-win solutions and for non-zero-sum games. We are most interested in organizations that empower, sustain, or regenerate their customers, communities, and environments while maintaining and even amplifying their own success. It is a model that transcends industries and provides insights for innovation and transformation everywhere, in agriculture and education as well as in retail, high tech, and beyond.

★ ★ ★

The COVID-19 pandemic will be a catalyst for a more distributed, more connected world and greater personal autonomy, a world of flow. The technologies that we needed to maintain some degree of "normalcy" were already in place for those companies and institutions, which were ready to adopt them. But now it's time for all of our companies and other institutions to catch up to our technologies. They need to take advantage of everything they offer, and to fully assimilate the various changes to work, leisure, shopping, worship, in short changes to just about all areas of our lives that the fear of another virus will drive and the evolution of technology will enable. To do that, they need to do the following.

They need to stop thinking of technology as a department. Instead they have to imagine themselves as "being" a kind of decentralized technology, a networked organization of connected, distributed, and autonomous agents (employees, customers, partners, other stakeholders). They need to enable remote or rather distributed working, and therefore they need to move all of their business processes and technologies to the cloud. They need to stop thinking about their customers being at the center of their organization and instead think about everyone being outside. And therefore they need to develop their customer-facing and relationship management systems and capabilities to become finely attuned to what's happening "out there" and to be able to respond with speed and intelligence. They need to reduce friction and increase delight for their customers by fully embracing mobile, voice, and virtual commerce. And they have to reimagine their identity, which means relying less on a physical location to create a sense of uniqueness and belonging and more on collective purpose and meaning to do so.

This is not to say that all forms of congregation are dead. Coming together to celebrate, play, worship is a deeply embedded need within us, a need that seems to predate even the first silo! And from that perspective the corporate office may become a place of occasional team learning, alignment, and celebration in its new role as a pump. But in a world of change, disruption, and uncertainty, centralization turns out to be a fragile model. Decentralization appears to be more resilient and more in tune with the needs of individuals as well as companies for success. The next normal is decentralization.

5 | Integration

Aligned Purpose + Value/s | Orchestration + Choreography | Circularity

"It's like Einstein said, it's easy to discover the theory of relativity; all you have to do is ignore a few basic axioms. What are they [in education]? One axiom is that you should separate kids by social class. We don't do that. You should separate those who are trained to use their heads from those who are trained to use their hands. You should segregate those who are going to college from those not going to college. You should segregate the school from the community like the old citadels from the twelve hundreds. Those are really old notions you know and so we just basically ignore all those things."
—*Larry Rosenstock, CEO High Tech High Schools (2009)*

What does it mean to be a company in a digital-first, decentralized world? What provides that sense of belonging when the physical manifestation of the company, the office, and its signage has been replaced by a loose confederacy of individual homes, coffee shops, cars, and other workplaces of the future? And what distinguishes one company from any other or from the "ecosystem" or from its own customers or competitors? The answer is Integration: integration of identity and purpose through an aligned workforce, integration of mission and the jobs-to-be-done through orchestration and choreography, integration of knowledge and value through the end-to-end and circular integration of customer journeys and data. The more Boundless the company becomes the closer the two principles of Connection and Integration become, but there will always be some distinction between the company and its surroundings; otherwise, it will simply merge into them and cease to exist per se. And yet this distinction is not a border, not a wall, not an impermeable barrier. It is instead an ongoing work-in-progress, a continuous effort or efforts by the company to maintain integration internally and connectedness externally. As the physiologist J. Scott Turner writes in *The Extended Organism: The Physiology of Animal-Built Structures* (2000), "It is not the boundary itself that makes an organism distinctive, but what that boundary does. In other words, the boundary is not a thing, it is a process" (p. x). In this chapter we focus on that work of integration that a Boundless entity must do, and that work begins with alignment.

Alignment

However conscientious we are about building relationships of trust across our entire ecosystems (as we discussed in Chapter 3), we still need to get to a shared understanding about the jobs to be done within our own companies and between them, and we need to be explicit about the why, how, and who of it all. We tend to assume that these sorts of things are handled by reporting structures, process methodologies, formal contracts between partners, and the like. Because we're so busy, and in the interests of time, we prefer to jump straight into our teamwork, our initiatives, programs, and projects, and to start making progress on them as quickly as possible.

We believe, however, that spending time up-front in setting initial conditions for success and taking an intentional and formal approach to gaining alignment—and then on a continuous basis—is essential to achieving that success.

It turns out that alignment is not one thing. We have identified six different aspects of alignment, each with its own specific purpose, approaches, and tools.

Purpose and Values

If there's one thing that creates a strong sense of identity for an organization it's having a clearly defined and articulated purpose and set of values, the things that are most important to the company and that inform and guide it in all its activities and decisions. This lets employees, customers, partners, and any other stakeholders know who they're doing business with, who they're in a relationship with, or are planning to be.

A good process can be used not only for organizational alignment, although that may be its core function, but also for any initiatives within it or for joint initiatives with ecosystem or community partners.

At Salesforce, we use a process known as the V2MOM (vision, values, methods, obstacles, and measures) that maps out all major corporate initiatives (known as methods) and aligns them to the company's vision and values. From there, in a cascading effect throughout the company, everyone has their own V2MOM that aligns their initiatives to their manager's V2MOM. All V2MOMs are accessible to everyone, including the CEO's, providing a level of transparency rare in large organizations. We also use the V2MOM structure for gaining alignment with our partners and customers at the programmatic level.

See the end of this chapter for a more detailed treatment of the V2MOM process.

Guiding Principles

In addition to purpose and values, it can also be useful to craft a guiding principle, just one question that can guide the choices in decisions and actions for all members of a program, team, department or business unit, or company as a whole. This is not the same as a company's North Star, vision, or mission statement, which typically has to distill a number of large and complex concepts into a sentence or two. The guiding principle is one question that gets to the heart of an initiative, a department or function, or a business.

Zappos makes it clear to all its employees that making the customer happy is the heart of the business. Service agents are famously not constrained by a script or by maximum call duration. Instead they have one goal: to make the customer happy. Their guiding principle is "Will it make the customer happy?" If yes, do it; if not, don't.

A successful question is one that team members can adopt easily and even ask themselves and each other out loud while making choices or decisions, creating a ritual that can help create team cohesion and sense of identity.

Will it make the boat go faster?

One of our favorite stories about alignment is the story of the Great Britain men's rowing team who in 1998, despite a steady string of mediocre performances in previous years, set their eyes on winning gold in the men's eight competition at the 2000 Sydney Summer Olympic Games. The story goes that the team came to a difficult conclusion. They could either keep on doing the same things in the same

ways they had for the previous seven or so years, in which case they
realized they would achieve exactly the same results, or they could
simply give up, or they could do things in an entirely different way.
They knew that they all shared the same crazy goal—gold in Sydney—
but that the goal itself was not enough to propel them forward. After
all, they had always competed to win but just weren't doing so. Their
breakthrough came when they realized that they could control some
things but not others. They could not control the performance of the
other teams, they couldn't control the conditions on race day, they
couldn't control what the public, the pundits, the press wrote or said
about them. They could, however, control the performance of their
own boat. Actually, more accurately, they could control their own
behaviors and actions that would affect their individual and collective
performance and the performance of the boat. They turned a crazy
dream into an understanding of the things they could control, and
they turned that understanding into a simple litmus test for all the
choices they made about their own behaviors. And that litmus test was
a single question: will it make the boat go faster? As told by one of the
members of that team, performance consultant Ben Hunt-Davis
(coauthor with Harriet Beveridge of the book *Will It Make the Boat
Go Faster? Olympic-Winning Strategies for Everyday Success*) they all asked
themselves the same question when deciding whether to go to the
pub or not, whether to go to bed early or not, whether to put the
extra work in on the rowing machine or not.

It was a particularly powerful question because it aligned everyone on a single desired outcome, one that they had significant control
over, and it gave each individual a guide for their own decision-
making even when no one else was around.

There is, of course, more to winning gold in the Olympics than
just following one principle as Hunt-Davis and Beveridge describe in
their book, but in many ways the single question encapsulates the
rest of it.

For best results the question needs to be a simple one—a yes-or-no question is best—and something a team can control through their own actions and behaviors. All companies and institutions and initiatives will have their own specific goals and desired outcomes, but as a general rule, for anyone wishing to model the Boundless paradigm, we think the following is a good start: "Will it increase the flow of value?"

Value Goals

Successful business relationships depend on the realization of mutual value. Companies need to understand the value that they want to realize from their relationships and what the value is that their customers and partners want to realize as well. Too often this definition of what constitutes value is left unstated and therefore assumed and can lead to problems later when the actual outcomes of a joint initiative or program or contract leave one or both parties unsatisfied. For that reason it is highly recommended that they align on the desired outcomes of the initiative (the value) ahead of time and define measures to assess progress.

Decision Rights

Within company hierarchies the decision rights in any given situation are often clear and default to the most senior person involved. But across those hierarchies, and especially across partner companies or ecosystem members, it is often much less clear who's accountable and who has decision rights for what. Models such as RACI (responsible, accountable, consulted, and informed) and RAPID (recommend, agree, perform, input, and decide) are very valuable in gaining alignment. It can feel like additional and even unnecessary bureaucracy up-front to spend the time on identifying the decisions to be made and the individuals with rights over them, but it can reduce friction and disagreement later on.

Ways of Working

Alignment needs to happen not only at the organizational level but also at the project level. In these cases it is also important to align on the methods, tools, and other constructs to be used and ensure everyone is up to speed on them. Teams should co-construct a list of desired and undesired work and communication styles.

Teaming Agreements

Teaming agreements go beyond the specific value, purpose, and outcomes of an initiative and focus instead on how everyone working on the initiative "shows up" for one another and the "rules of engagement" for the project. Teaming agreements can vary and should be cocreated by the team members together. Important agreements include these elements:

- **Disagreement handling.** Some types of friction can be productive—even generative—and others can be unproductive. The team needs to agree on how to enable and foster transparency, empowering everyone to bring their perspectives to bear even if they go against the grain. These perspectives deserve to be heard and considered as long as they are held with integrity and are consistent with the values of the organization.
- **Inclusivity.** It has long been recognized that people who are introverts by nature may not feel that they have opportunities to share their ideas and expertise in group settings. The team needs to agree on ways to ensure that all stakeholders are considered and all voices are heard.
- **Work-life balance.** Especially in difficult times such as the pandemic and in this "always-on" world of digital technologies, it is important to establish working and communication norms and expectations, including, for example, giving everyone the freedom to have notifications turned off outside established project hours.

Orchestration and Choreography

So far, we have shown that everything and everyone in the post-COVID world is going to become increasingly connected, increasingly decentralized, and increasingly autonomous. Employees are going to continue to work wherever they feel safe and productive, customers are going to continue to shop online and expect speedy home delivery. Students will do more of a mix of online and in-person learning, More and more services will be delivered remotely, cars will become autonomous, and robotaxis and drone delivery services will become the norm. Seniors will want to age in place, and telemedicine, connected health devices and concierge services both online and in home will support them.

For nearly all companies a big question is beginning to loom: how should they go about managing their resources in such a new world when they're actually designed for the exact opposite conditions? In this section we will focus on how they should go about managing their distributed employees, suggesting a new model based on the principle of Integration and on related technological advances.

The "Structure" of Management

In the old normal, management was conventionally a matter of hierarchy, not of expertise. An individual employee was the de facto manager of the employees directly beneath them in the company's org chart and a de facto subordinate of the employee above them in the same chart. The act or practice of management was never called out explicitly because it was taken for granted that the primary responsibility of the "owner" of each box on the chart was the management of everyone else in it. Likewise, nowhere on that org chart would we find "management" as a function, division, or department in the same way we would sales, marketing, or finance for example.

This hierarchy was supported and reinforced by the physical work-place. A manager, working from a private office, would oversee their direct reports working in the rank and file of cubicles outside their door, or would figuratively oversee them from a higher floor. In meetings it was an implicit but well-established practice that, depending on the lay-out of the room, the managers would sit at the place of greatest visibility, wherever they could see and be seen by their reports most clearly. There were rules to be followed, authorization and approvals to be gained, even etiquette and behavioral norms to be observed. And, of course, office attire, office hours, company signage, ID badges and security, the canteen, company communications and events all helped to establish belonging, or at least fit.

In the new normal, however, when the employees are working from home or indeed from anywhere, and when few of the old ways of establishing, demonstrating, and reinforcing hierarchy exist, the traditional command and control, direct supervision model of man-agement that was already creaking at the joints now feels significantly outdated. And although that sounds like a good thing, none of the old ways of establishing identity or belonging exist either, which sounds less good. Meanwhile, research has identified a correlation between employee experience (EX), customer experience, and growth:

> The study found that companies that were hyperfocused on enhanc-ing their employee engagement ultimately had higher customer engagement levels and revenue growth. More specifically, these com-panies amassed 1.8 times more revenue growth (nearly double) than organizations that solely focused on customers. Conversely, the respondents indicated that solely focusing on customers did not cor-relate to higher EX or revenue. (Bova, 2020)

In short, it may be more difficult than ever for management to focus on the employee experience, but it's also demonstrably more important than ever.

Orchestration

So, what can companies and their leadership do? Because the new normal is still so, well, new, there are no tried-and-true examples of distributed employee management. There are, however, analogs and precursors that might be productive. We asked ourselves if there are any other types of resources that are already based on Boundless principles—distributed, autonomous, connected, and mobile—and the most compelling example we came up with was autonomous vehicles. We then saw that for all the autonomous vehicles that are privately and individually owned there are also emerging models, such as mobility as a service (MaaS), where they are managed as fleets. And when we looked at the way these fleets of autonomous vehicles are being managed, what we found was the world of orchestration. Put simply, orchestration is the integration of distributed, autonomous resources.

Resource orchestration and service orchestration are already established practices in the world of software, where "the goal of orchestration is to streamline and optimize frequent, repeatable processes. Companies know that the shorter the time to market, the more likely they'll achieve success. Anytime a process is repeatable, and its tasks can be automated, orchestration can be used to optimize the process in order to eliminate redundancies" (Watts, 2020).

Mulesoft, the world's leading software integration platform, further defines the goals and the benefits of application orchestration as follows:

> Application or service orchestration is the process of integrating two or more applications and/or services together to automate a process, or synchronize data in real-time....Application orchestration provides (a) an approach to integration that decouples applications from each other, (b) capabilities for message routing, security, transformation and reliability and (c) most importantly, a way to manage and monitor your integrations centrally. (Mulesoft, n.d.)

So when we're talking about the management of digital resources in contemporary enterprises—where we want to maintain individual resource autonomy and yet still coordinate a great many of them toward a common goal—orchestration is already a key principle. Orchestration *is* integration, but—critically—it is not point-to-point or hard-wired integration, which creates dependencies and inflexibility. Orchestration is **dynamic** integration that creates almost endless opportunities for reuse and reconfiguration. Orchestration is circular (as we'll discuss later on).

Fleet orchestration is a logical extension of this principle. (We're still applying it to software, but this time to software that controls physical resources, such as cars, buses, and other vehicles, whose primary function is mobility—travel and transportation—rather than information processing.) These vehicles are called **autonomous** because they no longer rely on a human operator or driver and instead are controlled by this embodied software, being mostly sensor or AI based.

In some ways fleet orchestration is not so new. Taxi schedulers and distribution companies have been faced with the challenges of resource allocation and journey optimization for years or even decades. In the world of MaaS, however, fleet managers will need to handle far higher volumes with mixed demand types, mixed resources types, and with far more complex requirements for integration with external entities (such as automotive manufacturers, mapping companies, regulatory entities, and payment infrastructures), as well as with individual and business customers in on-demand and scheduled settings.

For example, Bestmile, a transportation software startup acquired in late 2021 by ZF (a €40 billion global technology company enabling the next generation of mobility), developed a fleet orchestration platform that, according to the company at the time, "can manage autonomous and human-driven vehicles, supports on-demand and fixed-route systems, integrates with multiple transport modes, and provides flexible applications for travelers, drivers, and operators. Its AI-powered algorithms orchestrate fleets with ultra-efficient ride matching, dispatching and routing proven to move more people with fewer vehicles with predictable operator and passenger KPIs" (Gindrat, 2019).

The benefits of fleet orchestration can be enormous. "Our [Best-mile] study found that 400 shared vehicles could do the work of 2700 Chicago taxis with predictable ride times and wait times. An MIT study found that a fleet of 3,000 taxis could meet 98 percent of demand served by New York City's 13,000 vehicles with an average wait time of 2.7 minutes. UT found that one shared autonomous vehicle could replace 10 personal autos with wait times between a few seconds and five minutes" (Gindrat, 2019).

The question is, can this orchestration model extend to companies and the management of their own resources, human as well as digital?

Applying Orchestration to Human Resources

John Kao, chairman of the Institute for Large Scale Innovation, has come to a similar conclusion as we have about the need for change in organization and management paradigms:

> Unfortunately, our leadership playbooks often remain largely frozen in time, originally designed for the authority and control needed to keep industrial bureaucracies functioning efficiently. But we are in the midst of a fourth Industrial Revolution that requires agility, rapid innovation and fluid, networked organizational designs. The commandant must give way to the orchestrator, the machine to the network. (Kao, 2020)

Corporate IT departments are already beginning to reflect this shift. In the world of Agile and DevOps practices, teams are self-organizing and autonomous and they apply orchestration principles to their release activities. According to Digital.ai:

> With Release Orchestration, DevOps teams are able to model software delivery pipelines, coordinate automated tasks with manual work, integrate a variety of tools for building, testing, and deploying software, and use data to identify bottlenecks and areas for potential areas for improvement." (Digital.ai, n.d.)

And a small but increasing number of companies are applying the Agile philosophy to business functions outside of IT, including marketing, HR, legal, and beyond, leading toward what has been called *enterprise agility*. McKinsey has described the benefits of this approach, showing that employee engagement, customer satisfaction, and operational performance can all be improved by it in its paper "Enterprise Agility: Buzz or Business Impact?" (Aghina, 2020).

A key feature of Agile enterprises, according to the article, is that they "can quickly redirect their people and priorities toward value-creating opportunities. A common misconception is that stability and scale must be sacrificed for speed and flexibility. Truly Agile organizations combine both: a strong backbone or center provides the stability for developing and scaling dynamic capabilities" (Aghina, 2020).

Although we would go further than this and stress that the backbone itself needs to be flexible and that the entire business needs to become comfortable with inherent instability, the point about orchestration is nevertheless clear. Orchestration is the connector among the strategy and shared purpose of the organization as a whole, its customer-focused missions, and its autonomous resources. Putting this into practice will not be simple, and should itself follow an Agile process, starting with a very small subset of customers journeys.

A critical concept to note here is that the orchestration function is not supervisory in the traditional sense. Orchestrators are not hierarchically more senior than the teams executing the missions. They don't "own" the resources, the missions, or the customers. They are flow-based, rather than silo-based, in the sense that their performance metrics are based on customer success, speed, and throughput, not on the size of their budget or on the number of employees they manage.

As companies become more and more data driven, as AI takes an increasingly central role in the operations of a company, so orchestration and other related functions will become increasingly evident and important. As in the fleet orchestration example, we can expect to see planning and forecasting, performance tracking, and business intelligence become more central components of the organization's decision-making tool set along with orchestration itself.

Choreography

So far we have discussed orchestration as a new form of integration that is relevant to human, digital, and hybrid resources alike. Orchestration is integration or alignment that is directed by the organization toward its resources. Choreography is another aspect of integration or alignment that is different from orchestration in that choreography is peer-to-peer coordination on the part of teams and individual members without "central" direction. Taking an autonomous taxi company as a future example, any given taxi in the company's fleet may decide, based on its sensing functions, that it needs servicing and so takes itself out of circulation. That would be individual self-determination, or what is most commonly thought of as autonomy. The fleet scheduler re-running its algorithm to account for the unavailability of one car and giving the rest of the fleet updated directions would be orchestration. The fleet on the road communicating locally with one another as well as with all other local non-fleet traffic to keep each other at the smallest safe distance apart and to travel at the fastest collective speed possible would be choreography.

Choreography is peer to peer in the sense that no central authority "runs" or "executes" it. Each agent, thing, object, or unit has a function that it performs but its performance is contextually dependent on the performance of its neighboring agents, things, and so on. Choreography is a Boundless architecture or design, meaning that it works on systems that exhibit other Boundless principles and ideas. The first of those is the idea of many and small instead of few and large (as we saw briefly in distribution and will see again in continuity). The second is the principle of autonomy, meaning the autonomy of each individual resource within the many and the small, which also requires that they are connected. And increasingly we expect these many, small, autonomous resources to have mobility as well.

In addition to the future scenario of the autonomous taxi company just described, we see choreography at play in the Starlink satellite system or "constellation," as SpaceX describes it. Each Starlink satellite is autonomous, meaning it has local intelligence and the ability for instance to move to avoid other objects in their vicinity. There are currently (as of May 2023) more than 4,000 satellites in the constellation, with a total of 12,000 planned and with a possible increase in numbers of up to 42,000 in the future. Until recently the satellites communicated directly with ground stations but newer satellites in the constellation are able to communicate with their neighbors via laser which reduces the dependency on those ground stations.

More generally, we see choreography playing an increasingly important role as the Internet of Things (IoT) continues to evolve and transform multiple sectors. This will surely include consumer IoT such as the Smart Home, industrial IoT as part of Industry 4.0, Smart Cities, and Space 2.0, as we have briefly discussed.

By analogy we can also think of individual employees and teams as being autonomous agents in the Boundless world. Each has their own mission to perform, and that mission will have been set by the organization through the orchestration function we described. And yet how they perform it will be partly their own decision and partly in collaboration with and/or in situational awareness of one another. The Boundless organization needs to provide its employees and teams with the means to be aware of each other's efforts and to communicate and collaborate with them directly without having to depend on a centralized supervision or management function to do so for them. The distributed nervous system we mention in Chapter 4 should provide or support at least some of that choreographic capability.

Circularity

When talking about integration, it is common to see the term *end to end* applied to it. Though this term is somewhat open to interpretation, we mean the ability to pass all relevant information seamlessly from one step in a linear process to the next one, starting at the first step all the way through to the final one, thus enabling the process to achieve its desired goal.

End-to-end design is often considered to be leading practice in integration. And, in fact, having end-to-end integration in any of these areas certainly would represent a leap forward for many companies who have built, acquired, or otherwise been required to use multiple systems, many of which are stand-alone, duplicate, and/or point-solution oriented and which make the flow of data, process, and experience either impossible or extremely hard work. And yet, being Boundless goes even beyond end-to-end integration to enable and support end-to-start, cradle-to-cradle, or what is more commonly being described as circular integration.

In this section we briefly describe different but closely related forms of circularity.

Experience Circularity (Extend to Entice)

Most companies focus their efforts on designing that part of their customers' experience in which the customer is most directly engaged with them, the part where typically the company is providing the service for which the customer is paying. This is completely understandable, but years ago designers at Doblin Group, part of Deloitte Digital, realized that truly compelling experiences often start long before the actual engagement and they end long after it. They identified five stages of compelling experiences; entice, enter, engage, exit, extend. This five-stage model, the *5Es* as it is called, helps designers take a truly end-to-end perspective of a customer experience but goes further than that by imagining how the extension of one experience may lead to an enticement to engage in another, whether through repeating the same experience or trying out a different one.

As we discussed in Chapter 3, becoming Boundless encourages us to go beyond experience alone and to situate them within the context of relationships. After all, why go to the bother of designing a compelling experience for a customer if not in the hope of either forming a new relationship with them or nurturing and developing an existing one? We recognize that relationships have a beginning but they may not have either a middle or an end per se. Instead they exhibit circularity; they grow, mature, and evolve over time through multiple iterations of experiences and transactions.

Process Circularity (SUDA)

Sense and respond is an increasingly common theme for businesses. In our view, organizing for the ability to sense and respond is a hallmark of a Boundless organization. We focus on the similarities between sense and respond for business and for autonomous technologies in Chapter 10. Here we would simply note that the ability to sense and respond is important at every level in a business, from an individual employee to the organization as a whole, and from a real-time interaction with a customer to a product development process or a business cycle. The sense and respond model is not only circular, it is continuous and it is fractal.

Data Circularity

In the traditional view of data management the logic was that we should capture as much structured data as possible and then aggregate it all as far as possible to enable us to "slice and dice" it and generate summarized snapshots of historical activity. Or we should sell it. This has left many companies with huge amounts of data that they really don't know what to do with and that don't support real-time customer experiences and interactions. And, as we have mentioned previously, many companies manage hundreds of systems to support their business processes, many of which do not easily share data with one another. So we are left with silos of static, stand-alone data. And yet data is regarded as the lifeblood of the modern business. Much as blood flows around the body to deliver resources to wherever it's most needed and is refreshed by the lungs and pumped by the heart continuously, data needs to flow throughout the company to where it's most needed to support customer-facing processes and experiences as well as internal facing ones. And with the rapid rise in AI to support business processes and decision-making, the reuse of data is even more critical than ever before. AI feeds on transactional data and the more data it receives the better its algorithms become. Only after use and reuse in this way should the data then become part of the historical record for use in historical performance analysis and reporting, and in pattern and trend discovery.

Resource Circularity (Reuse, Recycle)

In our brief definition of an end-to-end integration we could also describe it as a linear process that starts with the input of a resource (which could be data in the form of a request from a potential customer or raw materials) and ends with a desired outcome (which could be the conversion of that inquiry into a sale or the conversion of that raw material into a physical consumer product). In this end-to-end view, at least when it comes to physical products, the design process stops at the conversion to the end product. What comes next, the life cycle of that product and its end of life, is rarely designed. Instead it is assumed that it will be eventually discarded as waste. The Ellen Macarthur Foundation (n.d.) defines this as the linear economy, the process of "take, make, waste." In its place, the foundation and an increasing number of entities is calling for the adoption of a circular economy. As with experience, process, and data circularity, we can design for the circularity of all resources, especially physical, finite resources. The circular economy follows three design principles:

- **Eliminate waste and pollution.** It is observed that nature creates no waste. Everything is reused by everything else. In the human-built world this means that we need to take an ecosystem view, as we discussed in Chapter 3, as well as an integration view. We need also to eliminate the silo-based perspective of "externalities" that enables not just manufacturing but all of our industries and sectors, including education and health care, to discard their by-products, failures, rejects, and dropouts without regard for their consequences on other parts of society or the environment.

- **Circulate products and materials.** The circular thinking that applies to process, experience, and data also applies to physical stuff. It all requires the same rethinking that recognizes the power of reuse and recycling and that extends the design envelope or scope beyond just engage and to extend and beyond. We are beginning to realize that our approach to data storage may have been misplaced and that the real power is in real-time "live" transaction data that can not only support customer experiences but also be fed back into machine learning and improve AI algorithms, as well as becoming the source of historical, trend-based information. As we saw with the eco-industrial park Kalundborg in Chapter 3, all "exhaust" can be redirected and harnessed in real time.

- **Regenerate nature.** We have already seen the power of regenerative agriculture to transform the oldest of our industries and create a replicable system that is better for the soil, the animals and plants, the farmers and their workers, customers, and nature. This is the goal of all Boundless entities. The focus of the circular economy on renewable energy sources—what we might call flow-based sources such as wind, wave, and solar—and on renewable materials is an important aspect of becoming Boundless.

To wrap up this portion: integration is the new headquarters. It is what differentiates one entity from another in the world of increasing digitization, decentralization, and connectedness. As siloed companies give rise to Boundless ecosystems, artificial boundaries between organizations will disappear and transparency between ecosystem members will increase dramatically. And yet, we know that successful relationships depend on mutual value and on a distinctive "personality." So individual companies, even the most advanced in terms of Boundlessness, need a personality, a difference, a reason for a relationship with them to form. Alignment of employees on a shared purpose, vision, and values creates that personality. The orchestration of distributed, autonomous resources, human, digital, and hybrid, creates that personality. The circularity of data, experiences, and processes, of all resources digital and physical, creates that personality.

Integration, Connection, and Alignment at Salesforce

How can you establish and strengthen connections in a structured and meaningful way? Is the process of establishing connections a mindset or a framework? Is there a tool that can be used to build connections?

As mentioned before, Salesforce uses a unique goal-setting process to strengthen employee-to-stakeholder connections, and it is called V2MOM—vision, values, methods, obstacles, and measures. Salesforce asks every employee to add a well-being goal to their V2MOM plan because shared success is part of the winning formula.

The V2MOM consists of five questions, which create a framework for alignment and leadership. It is important to note that long-lasting connections are based on strong alignments and shared core values and execution principles. The V2MOM five questions are as follows:

1. Vision—what do you want?
2. Values—what's important to you?
3. Methods—how do you get it?
4. Obstacles—what is preventing you from being successful?
5. Measures—how do you know you have it?

According to Marc Benioff, inventor of the V2MOM, the framework provides a detailed map of where the company is going and also serves as a compass to direct the workforce. The process is revisited annually and it starts with a blank sheet of paper.

In Benioff's (2019) book *Trailblazer: The Power of Business as the Greatest Platform for Change* (cowritten with Monica Langley), they write,

> Starting with a beginner's mind we could declutter our minds, dispose of outdated assumptions, eliminate distractions, and allow ourselves to focus on what, why, and how of whatever we set out to do. Moreover, memorializing it on paper would make it far easier to get everyone aligned. We needed to all be in the same boat, rowing in the same direction, and looking out for the same rocks and shoals that could sink our boat to have any chances of arriving safely in port with our cargo.

The V2MOM has developed principles that speak to strengthening connections. To begin, everything has to be ranked in order of priority. Every word matters. And last, the plan has to be simple (not simplistic) so that it can be remembered and easily understood.

Benioff explained:

> The V2MOM became the perfect framework for engaging our beginner's mind approach to business planning. Articulating our vision kept us grounded in reality, while writing down our values kept us in touch with our guiding principles. Naming our obstacles forced us to honestly confront what was holding us back, and quantifying what success looks like kept us honest—to ourselves and to one another. The V2MOM would prove to be our most important management tool, guiding every decision at Salesforce and setting our uniform course for the entire company as we went from four hundred people to forty thousand we have today.

Benioff points to the simplicity of the V2MOM and beauty of its application to all phases of the organization's life cycle. The framework also extends beyond the individual to the entire organization and its ecosystem. The V2MOM is written by every single Salesforce employee, cascading up and down the entire company. And the most powerful aspect of the V2MOM framework is that it is shared with the entire company. This open book approach means every single V2MOM, written by every single employee, is accessible to all employees. The radical transparency of creation, distribution, and use as a compass that is open to every single employee.

"I've found that the V2MOM process can help navigate a relationship. Working together to identify our vision and values as a team helped us see how our skills could complement each other. I am not sure how many of our employees have made the connection between the V2MOM process and the notion of mindfulness. But over the years, it's become clear to me that the true power in this exercise is maintaining a beginner's mindset throughout the V2MOM process," said Benioff.

Strong connections are established and maintained with deliberate intentions of benefits of mutuality. To better understand the needs of yourself and your connections you must be deliberate and aligned on a vision, common set of values, and the necessary steps to get there. Relationships are based on trust and alignment of interests. In order to build relationships and strong connections we must be clear about our intentions, commitments, and goals. The methods and measurements of the V2MOM process enable us to share our approach toward adding value to our connections. We also promise to measure our efforts, and most importantly the outcomes, in order to demonstrate accountability and commitment to shared success.

And last, the process of prioritizing the V2MOM content is a forcing function for us to focus on what matters most to us and our connections. If everything is a high priority, then nothing is a high priority. Every word on the V2MOM document is measured, calculated, and recognized in the order of importance. This process is deliberate, measured, transparent, flexible, adaptive, and reoccurring.

Strong connections require continuous work—often hard work that is mindful, empathetic, transparent, deliberate, proactive, prioritized, and intentional. The work must be documented, communicated, refined, and shared continuously. Connections are not a destination, but a journey. A journey of optimism, hope, unselfish generosity, humility, and a beginner's mindset—hungry, inquisitive, and free of prejudice.

We believe that a good way to start establishing and keeping connections is for you to develop your own V2MOM-like process. Cocreate it, share it, continuously review, and modify it, and do not forget to celebrate its positive outcomes every step of the way. And, finally, remember that the best teacher is your last mistake. So if the V2MOM framework highlights mistakes in your approach to establish connections, do not be timid about refining or changing the plan. Smart people often change their minds. Which means that your V2MOM will constantly change. This is normal given your connection's needs and wants also constantly change. What will remain somewhat steadfast are your core values.

6 | Autonomy

AI | Learning | Identity

"*The illiterate of the future are not those who can't read or write but those who cannot learn, unlearn, and relearn.*"
—*Alvin Toffler*, Future Shock *(1970)*

In a silo, resources are stripped of all their support systems that they would have enjoyed on the "outside" and are heavily controlled on the inside. The resources become dependent on the silo owner for direction and for support and are there only for their productivity. Compliance and rule-following is rewarded and more highly prized than creativity or innovation.

Boundless entities empower their resources—which in the business world are primarily employees—to make decisions and act in keeping with their unified mission, plan, or purpose and with customer success as the primary goal. They support and empower their customers' autonomy, as well as that of their employees, through their experiences, offerings, and organizational models. And, increasingly, the technology that is available to companies is developing its own autonomy, in large part thanks to the huge advances that have been made, and are continuing to be made, in artificial intelligence (AI).

Once again, then, companies are at a turning point. Do they embrace the autonomy of their customers, employees, and technologies, or do they resist it? In this chapter we want to take a closer look at autonomy and AI and to explore what this means for companies. In particular we want to consider how companies support the autonomy of their human and digital resources by becoming *learning* companies.

Meanings of Autonomy

Autonomy covers a wide range of meanings. At a human level, autonomy means the power of self-governance or self-determination—the ability and freedom to make decisions for oneself and to act on them. But it can also take on more context-specific meanings. In the workplace, for instance, autonomy tends to mean the ability of the individual employee to decide for themselves how to perform the tasks expected of them, and then their ability to actually perform them without direct supervision, as long as they do so in keeping with the organization's goals, values, and overall mission. And from a consumer or customer perspective, they've always had the freedom to make decisions for themselves at least in principle but technology has given them increasing connection, information, choice, and influence, all of which greatly contribute to their sense of autonomy or self-determination in practice. This also means that companies can no longer treat their customers as interchangeable members of a mass market. They have to respect their autonomy and their individuality.

For technological systems, autonomy in its broadest definition means the ability to perform a task expected of it without direct human supervision. This definition, however, covers a very broad spectrum of abilities and task complexities. At one end of the scale we have robots that execute pre-programmed, repetitive tasks independently and other machines such as drones that are operated and controlled by humans but remotely. At the other end of the scale—recognizing, of course, that the technology is always evolving and that therefore the degree of autonomy demonstrated by technology is always increasing—we have software that is situationally and dynamically aware, that can handle high levels of complex decision-making in real time, and that can learn. This type of software may be integrated with hardware to form autonomous systems such as self-driving cars, or it may operate without it as programs, such as AlphaGo Zero, the strongest player of Go—human or computer—in history, or such as the increasingly powerful chatbots that enable real time e-commerce at immense scale. At this end of the scale, autonomy is dependent on AI, as we will discuss a little later.

Next-Generation Human Autonomy

In this next portion Henry shares a story of slime.

In spring 2017, I was leading a "future of education" project, one of the highlights of which was the first ever blockchain prototype in the higher education space. Exciting as this was, I found my imagination caught by a much lower tech development: slime. My project partner and my client each had two young daughters, and all four girls were caught up in a craze that literally stretched far and wide: making highly tactile slime from a combination of white school glue (like Elmer's) and borax (although safer recipes include ingredients like baking soda and saline solution).

What made the slime craze so interesting was not really the slime but the nature of the craze itself. This was not an advertising-fueled fad centered on a commercially owned and controlled product like Webkinz but a grassroots, influencer-driven movement. It exploded from obscurity in 2016 and catapulted a few influencers like Karina Garcia, "the Queen of Slime," to fame and fortune almost overnight, with her YouTube videos routinely getting 10 to 20 million views (e.g., Connley, 2018). But the heart of the craze was the kids themselves—mainly girls, but some boys, too. They bought out the nation's supply of white school glue (e.g., Strain, 2017), made and watched each other's DIY slime videos on YouTube, broadcast real-time demos using Instagram Live, and even bought and sold slime on Etsy. It was simultaneously a highly tactile, very traditional communal practice and an ultra-modern, online phenomenon that engaged millions and spread internationally. And it was Boundless in its organization, its reach, and its spirit of exploration and magic.

Eventually of course, the thing did get productized. Elmer's itself started to sell slime kits in 2017 (Sleeper, 2018) as did Karina, who was able to secure partnerships with huge brands including Coca-Cola and Target (Connley, 2018). But the moral of this story is not just about companies being slow to respond to what their customers and their markets are up to (although, of course, it's that, too!). What's really at play here is the future of work. You see, the girls in this story were neither "playing" nor "consuming," at least not in the traditional definitions of those words. Rather, they were designing and developing and marketing products; they were buyers and sellers, directors, distributors, and stars of online entertainment and video training materials; they were content producers, e-commerce developers, and storefront owners. In short, as 10- to 14-year-olds they were already building practical experience in nearly every business discipline as we understand it today. And they were doing it all themselves. Of course, there were parents supervising in some of the kitchens/laboratories around the world, but by and large the girls were experimenting and learning by themselves and for themselves, sometimes individually and other times with friends. They built a body of knowledge, built skills, and experienced a kind of autonomy that they are unlikely to forget.

We are living in a time when young people are more connected to each other and more connected to new capabilities and new potentialities than ever before, all thanks to technologies that will keep evolving—and companies are starting to look slow and out of touch in comparison. In just a few years these enterprising girls will complete their formal education and join the workforce. When they do, they will come armed with all this experience and more—and they're most likely not going to be interested in taking entry-level positions in companies that have whole departments dedicated to just one of those disciplines.

Our current generation of business leaders—and not just in HR but in marketing and new product development, in engineering, and basically all across the board—have maybe five years to figure out a solution to this unprecedented problem. How do we reconfigure our businesses to attract and empower the future workforce, given that their individual capabilities and self-determination, empowered by digital technologies are now as great as ours? To answer this question, we first have to connect with that workforce and those emerging technologies to understand precisely what they're becoming capable of—and to do so as keenly we must connect with our customers, partners, and other stakeholders (for many of the same reasons).

Next-Generation Technological Autonomy

Crew Dragon Demo-2, the NASA/SpaceX flight carrying two astronauts to the International Space Station (ISS) on May 30, 2020, marked a return, after nearly a decade, of the US's ability to send astronauts to space under its own terms and from within its own borders. It was also the first time any private company has launched people into orbit. We are transitioning into a new era in spaceflight. But what does that really mean? What's so new about it? And what, if anything, can more terrestrially minded companies learn from it about the future?

Floating in a tin can?

To answer the question of what's so new about it: the clearest signs, beyond ownership and control, were in the changing relationship between astronaut and spacecraft. We have become used to thinking of astronauts as death-defying heroes. They not only head out into the unknown but they do it atop a barely controlled explosive device containing, as those of us who followed the Apollo program like to think, less computing capacity than our mobile phones have. The rocket was like a dragster: fast, dumb, and wild. The archetypal astronaut was its driver, cool under pressure, brave, measured, able to thread the needle between optimal performance and near certain catastrophe—essentially a risk whisperer. Similar to a champion downhill skier (though heading in the opposite direction) neither quite in control nor quite out of control either.

But this launch was not that, despite the obvious similarities and continuities. There was a rocket, certainly, on the same launchpad, 39A at NASA's Kennedy Space Center, where NASA launched the *Apollo* and space shuttle missions. And there was *Endeavour*, named by the astronauts to the *Dragon* spacecraft as a clear link to the last space shuttle ever built and that both astronauts had flown.

As the launch progressed, however, and we were able to watch it unfold thanks to a video camera giving us a backseat view, the difference became clear. The astronauts were as comfortable in their rocket ship as in the Tesla Model X that delivered them to the launchpad. The vehicle went about its business and did all the work, smoothly, efficiently, quietly, nominally. Its passengers sat there, safely buckled in, obviously enjoying the ride.

By the time *Dragon* reached the ISS, it felt like the extreme rigors and risks of spaceflight had been replaced by something safer, something perhaps achievable by mere mortals. Chris Cassidy, the NASA astronaut already onboard the ISS who greeted them, said, "When we got that hatch open, you could tell it was a brand-new vehicle, with smiley faces on the other side, [a] smiley face on mine—just as if you had bought a new car, the same kind of reaction. Wonderful to see my friends and wonderful to see a brand-new vehicle" (Weltering, 2020). Just a couple of dudes, showing off their dope new ride to an old buddy!

From launch until their return journey to Earth nearly 64 days later, on August 2, 2020, all tests showed that *Dragon* performed beyond expectations. It was fully autonomous for the duration of the journey, except during two early manual tests, doing its job of delivering the astronauts to the ISS and enabling them to do theirs.

★ ★ ★

Elon Musk is the visionary behind both Tesla and SpaceX, and autonomy is a core component of his vision for the future. Nearly all of the technologies he develops are designed to be, or become, autonomous, from the Tesla cars on earth to the growing constellation of Starlink satellites and the *Dragon* in orbit. And if all goes well, the *Dragon* will be succeeded by the still more powerful starship, capable of delivering up to 100 people at a time to the moon, Mars, and beyond.

The autonomous vehicle in many ways provides us with a glimpse into the future of business—the autonomous enterprise. In the future, the combination of technologies such as machine learning and deep learning, computer visioning, smart robotics, natural language processing, sensors and wearable technologies, digital smart assistants, and spatial computing with augmented and virtual reality will create a highly automated and autonomous set of capabilities. Future business applications will anticipate, recommend, and in many cases fully deliver value at the speed of their stakeholders' needs.

AI and Autonomy

Decision-making is essential to human autonomy—so much so that we tend to take for granted the intelligence that enables our decision-making, along with the learning that improves it. By contrast, few of us take for granted the marvels of AI. Indeed, the impact of the evolution of technological intelligence is so immense that we might face a new crisis in the near future. Does AI represent an existential risk to humanity, or will it help take our species to the next level? No one yet knows the answer, but as optimists we believe that AI is key to higher-level technological autonomy—and that autonomy is key to a Boundless future for organizations and individuals alike.

There is a general agreement about how these higher-level autonomous systems work. We cover this in more detail in Chapter 10, because we think that the organization of the future will need to be similar to an autonomous technology system. But in brief, these systems have four main capabilities: sense, understand, decide, act. They sense changes in their environment, they understand the impact of those changes on them and the choices they have to deal with them, they decide from among those choices, and they act on that decision. Their action leads immediately back to sensing, and the loop repeats in real time until they have completed their mission. All autonomous systems are capable of acting. Most have sensing capabilities as well though at various different levels of sophistication and power. But only systems with AI are capable of understanding and deciding.

As we discussed previously, AI can work with hardware or as part of a program or potentially both. In the former category, AI is an essential component of an autonomous vehicle, enabling it to understand everything that is going on around it (which it learns through its sensors) and to decide how to act accordingly (through the vehicle's steering, accelerating, and/or braking functions) in order to reach its destination safely. In the latter category we have already seen how Alibaba uses AI to become a "smart company" (see Chapter 3), and OpenAI's ChatGPT is probably the best-known generalized AI tool currently available. As a sign of the increasing interest in AI not just at the corporate level but also among individuals, ChatGPT reached over 1 million users in just its first five days after launch in November 2022, according to Mira Murati, the company's chief technology officer.

★ ★ ★

We hinted earlier that autonomous systems are not only intelligent but that they enhance their intelligence through learning. This is achieved in AI primarily through machine learning in which the AI's algorithms are typically refined by running them against the largest datasets available. This is true both for "hardware-embodied" and application-based AI.

Tesla has built its own supercomputer, Dojo, specifically for the purposes of AI machine learning. The company is connected to its entire fleet of over 1 million cars on the road around the world and uploads video data from them as its dataset. Dojo trains the full self-driving (FSD) AI program using the data and then downloads it to the 160,000 or so cars that are currently beta testing FSD.

The world of Go, the strategy board game first played in China more than 2,500 years ago, was transformed forever in March 2016 when the AlphaGo program developed by DeepMind Technologies beat Lee Sedol, a 9-dan Go player and one of the very best players in the world, by four games to one. AlphaGo (as well as later versions called AlphaGo Master, AlphaGo Zero, Alpha Zero, MuZero and now EfficientZero) learned by playing against itself. AlphaGo Zero learned the game without any human datasets at all (i.e., without learning from games that human experts had already played) and within just three days had beaten AlphaGo, the version that defeated the best human in the world, 100 games to 0.

And in the world of e-commerce we have already seen how Alibaba is on a mission to "software" and "datafy" everything. It believes that data, real-time or live transactional data, is fundamental to the ability of the company and the entire ecosystem to grow. This is not a case of building massive warehouses of historical data but rather of directing a steady flow of data through the ecosystem to make it smarter and smarter over time. It will be the smartness of the ecosystem, not the size, that will enable it to scale to meet the needs of billions.

If technology gets better through continuous learning then companies should as well, through the collective and individual learning of its employees and partners. We still have a dominant culture of batching up education before joining the workforce (and then batching up work until retirement!) but some leaders in the education sector and in business/industry have recognized the potential of applying Agile or flow-based approaches to learning. This includes learning in smaller chunks than the traditional four-year undergraduate degree and rewarding it with badges and micro-credentials. It also includes nontraditional learning pathways as well as lifelong learning. The point is that learning and working can often be intertwined instead of separated. Learning is a way of refreshing an employees' skills and capabilities and increasing both their value and their sense of being valued.

Beyond this, a few organizations have recognized that investing in the education of not only their own employees but in that of their partners and customers and communities can transform those relationships and build the ecosystem's resilience. Boundless companies will look for ways to enhance their customers' autonomy and transform them into superheroes by providing them with the best possible learning as well as the best possible products and services.

Identity and Autonomy

In the discussion of autonomy we also need to reflect on the issues of online data ownership and digital identity that may soon change the digital world as we know it—and may even make it a better place.

Obviously, the internet is no longer a phenomenon. Being connected digitally is quickly becoming part of what it means to be human. Of the 8 billion people now populating the world, well over half of us are internet users and two-thirds of us are mobile users. Our work lives and our social lives are increasingly spent online—a trend hugely accelerated by the COVID-19 pandemic—and before long it will be hardly an exaggeration to suggest that the digital or virtual world, the world of bits, is as "real" as the analog or physical one, the world of atoms. And that digital world is growing faster, in terms of connections and content, as well as in ways of experiencing that content.

But there's a problem—most of us are missing!

But as this world has grown since the new millennium or so, something strange has happened to us. If we are our bodies and our stuff in the world of atoms, then we are our data in the world of bits. But our data is all over the place, captured, stored, and duplicated across multiple sites and servers that we neither own nor even necessarily know about. Very few of us have coherent online identities— and even those who do, such as social media personalities and influencers, aren't in control of them. We have to log in to nearly everywhere we go, which means that the companies that own the sites or applications we log in to also own our data—and given that identity or self in the digital world *is* data, that means they own us. We simply do not have identity or presence in the online world as free individuals. We are missing from the world we created. This has created a range of problems:

Identity theft. When our identities—our data—become commodities, we become targets for thieves and unscrupulous practices, and a whole industry has grown up to trade those commodities. Of course, most companies with whom we interact usually have the best intentions when they capture our data, but trust is a major issue for 95% of all customers, both business and consumer, because we have no control over what these companies do with "us."

Privacy and anonymity. Some people, especially the younger generations, share even their most mundane moments with the rest of the world. Others, however, are less comfortable playing out their lives in public and would like to be able to keep their preferences and predilections to themselves. Privacy and anonymity solutions may well become a major opportunity for entrepreneurs going forward.

Massive (messy) data. We all have multiple online IDs and passwords and multiple accounts and profiles, each of which store their own version of our address, credit card information, shopping history, and so on. There is a lot of data out there about us, much of which is inaccurate and incomplete. And even the most fastidious of companies end up battling redundant and duplicate records and multiple IDs assigned by various systems that have no integration and no single "source of truth." Data cleanup is an ongoing, expensive, and irritating task for companies and customers alike.

Sluggish innovation. We're seeing a bottleneck in the rate and scope of innovation because we're using the wrong metaphor for the online world. The idea of self and individual identity got left behind sometime in the dotcom era of the "eyeball economy," and since then the close coupling of self and site, or self and app, has limited the range of online products, services, and experiences that could be designed for us. (For more, see the upcoming "Emergent Opportunities" section.)

Digital Identities

So, what to do? If we *are* our data in the digital world, then we need a new kind of digital entity to bring together, store, and look after that data, including financial, health, education, and social. In essence, this entity would be our digital self, representing us in the world of sites and apps as individuals and coordinating interactions with third parties (those sites and apps) and other "selves" on behalf of our physical self. It would grow and evolve continuously over time as our experiences, relationships, and learnings do likewise. This digital self is not the same thing as an avatar, which need bear no resemblance to us in any respect; nor is it a digital assistant, like Siri or Alexa, which is a third-party-owned interface. We would all have our own individual selves, which we would own directly and access readily—without needing to gain permission first.

In order to make this happen we will need to migrate from an application-centered architecture for the web to a "personal" one in which we—our personal data—are decoupled from third-party sites and applications. This is, of course, how it happens in the physical world. It would be absurd to say that we belong to the coffee shop that we're sitting in or to the bar where we meet up with friends. And yet when we're at the bar we do recognize the right of the establishment to check our IDs, as well as to keep its own records of our visit there, including what we ate and drank, and when. Our new model will continue to recognize the right for sites like Meta to capture data about the time we spend visiting each other in their space. But they don't get to keep our financial data. They don't get to keep our photos and other personal property that we brought with us. That should not be how either world works.

★ ★ ★

This is not a brand-new idea of course, and the problem of an application- or site-centered web has been known for a long time. Sir Tim Berners-Lee, the "father" of the world wide web, has always been troubled by how his invention has come to be built (e.g., Field, 2020). He collaborated with MIT on a "web decentralization" project called Solid (derived from "social-linked data," solidproject .org) that has at its heart this goal of digital identity data application decoupling. The project is mostly focusing on the design and conventions necessary to share one's social data in a modular and extensible way while still maintaining true ownership of said data. Berners-Lee has now spun the Solid project out into a company called Inrupt whose technology "puts individuals in control of their data, gives organizations new opportunities to create value for customers, and allows developers to thrive in an open marketplace of innovation" (Hale, 2022).

Of course, Berners-Lee is not alone in this effort, and there are now numerous companies engaged in developing solutions for digital identity, or self-sovereign identity as it is sometimes also called. If they are successful they will have built a decentralized foundation that truly redefines our concept of the web and of the internet as a whole. With these technologies all working in concert, our digital selves can exist within our own secure network and at the same time be shared across the wide array of decentralized applications and services that we allow. This approach is literally flipping the script on the way we think about our online existence today.

Emergent Opportunities

Innovations involving decoupling have long created new opportunities with major scaling impacts. About 1440, Johannes Gutenberg developed the printing press, which decoupled text (the data) from the book (the application) and created the first mass reproduction and accessibility of knowledge. Nearly 400 years after that the invention of interchangeable (premanufactured) parts—popularized most notably by Eli Whitney with the construction of muskets—decoupled function from function, part from whole, and ushered in the world of industrial, mass production of just about everything.

So we should expect an equivalent explosion to be unleashed by the decoupling of self from application. This will manifest in changes to existing solutions and in the development of brand-new ones.

Existing e-commerce sites and social media applications will need to be reconfigured to communicate with our digital self. Even enterprise systems, such as customer relationship management, will need to be re-architected to embrace a new, dynamic, and evolving "single source of truth" that comes from the customers themselves—a radical departure from current solutions. The change will affect any and all places where our data is stored, including, for example, educational credentials, government petitions, health care claims histories, support for elderly care, personal résumés, and so on.

New solutions will include the design and development of the digital self and architecture itself as well as a whole new set of applications and/or other digital entities to manage, protect, and serve it, and new and emerging sets of standards and protocols to enable and support these distributed apps. When we have a digital self and a physical one we will need to take care of it, groom it, and enable it to reflect and represent us appropriately. We will be able to, and will need to, ensure that our selves are coherent, that we are equally trustworthy online and "in person," and that our goals in both worlds are consistent with each other. Whereas existing virtual worlds may enable us and even encourage us to escape our real selves, new solutions built for the personal web paradigm will enable us to coordinate and maximize the potential of our selves and the worlds we build.

All new paradigms provide brand-new opportunities for those who understand them. The emergence of personal computing gave us Microsoft and Apple. The first five years of the world wide web gave us Google and Amazon. The world of apps exploded from nothing in 2008 with the launch of the iPhone and the App Store. The emergence of the personal web and digital self, one in which we can reclaim our identities while still engaging in, and rewarding appropriately, experiences and connections that we value, will provide opportunities big and small for developers and other entrepreneurs. Many of today's most successful apps will need to be rewritten to accommodate data ownership. But this does not mean that they will fail. Meta, LinkedIn, and other social sites will still provide a great service to people as online meeting places. Chances are that sharing will actually become more prevalent, not less, when it's always possible to reclaim one's data and one's self.

Tomorrow's Symbiotic Autonomy

We think the company of the future will be like an autonomous spaceship or car. It will be powered by AI and other digital technologies that increase the speed and relevance of the company to customer needs. It will free us from clerical and other repetitive tasks that, frankly, we're not very good at, and it will help us make better, faster decisions and take better, faster actions. It will force us, in a good way, to refocus on our human qualities, such as our abilities to imagine and create brand-new products, experiences, solutions, and other forms of value, and our ability to have empathy for others and to build relationships of trust with them. It will require us to respect and nurture the autonomy of our employees and to respect all of our unique identities, in the digital and physical worlds alike.

In some ways we're not so far off. We already use technology to support many of our business processes. But we're still responsible for the driving, and our corporate senses are just not nearly as attuned to our customers and the markets as they need to be. We still have accidents—"collisions" with our customers or partners—that could be avoided with better sensing capabilities and with faster, more effective decision-making.

The company of the future will be a new type of symbiotic organization of autonomous technology and autonomous humans, working effectively together, accelerating the flow of value, as and when needed, to our customers and all other stakeholders in the ecosystem.

7 | Mobility

Flow | Mobile Technologies | Environments

"The most profound technologies are those that disappear. They weave themselves into the fabric of everyday life until they are indistinguishable from it."

—Mark Weiser, CTO Xerox PARC (1991)

Given that movement is life and vice versa, movement and success go hand in hand. We describe someone who's doing well as being on the move, on their way up, moving and shaking, really going places. By contrast, those who aren't doing so well are often thought of as being stuck or bogged down, at a standstill and getting nowhere.

And it's not just metaphorical. As individuals, our relationship to movement really does help to define where we fit in the social pecking order, from least to most fortunate; at one end of the spectrum are those with little or no control over their own movement or that of anyone else. This includes those who are denied movement, such as prison inmates; those who are unable to move themselves, such as the severely disabled; and also those who, conversely, are forced to move, such as migrant workers and the victims of human trafficking. And at the other end are those who can choose to stay or to go, who can summon others to them, and who show off their control over movement through ownership and collection of its most extravagant and luxurious symbols: exotic cars, thoroughbred horses, super-yachts, and private planes. And in between are all sorts of subtle clues regarding rank provided by mode and duration of daily commute, number and type and age of cars owned, ownership of a passport, number of foreign countries visited, distance traveled on vacation, frequent flier status, and so on almost endlessly.

Beyond success, we protect the freedom to move as a fundamental human right, and we are coming to regard movement as essential to wellness and to longevity. With each dam that is removed in the US it is reported that life returns to the river almost as soon as it starts to flow again. And it is only when blood stops flowing through our bodies that we are pronounced clinically dead.

Flow in Action

So you'd be forgiven for thinking that movement, or flow, would be a basic design principle of everyday experiences such as shopping,

145

working, learning, getting medical attention, traveling, and so on. And yet the exact opposite happens to be true. Organizations of all types take their customers, employees, students, patients, members, and guests out of their flow and bring them to a standstill, figuratively and literally, simply because, from the organizations' perspective, having customers wait in line or on "hold" on the phone is the easiest, cheapest, or most obvious way to handle them. We may be living in a fast-moving world, but we spend a lot of time in it sitting or standing still.

And yet it doesn't have to be that way. There are examples all around us of companies that are realizing the importance of replacing the traditional static model that optimizes for organizational convenience with a new dynamic that optimizes for effective experiences. And the reason to take this seriously is that experiences that prioritize the movement or flow of individuals nearly always delivers the dual benefits of increasing customer success (they accomplish whatever they set out to do with greater speed and less friction) while simultaneously reducing operational costs—often improving their environmental or community impact as well. And, because this is by no means the norm in any industries or sectors, organizations that design for movement are highly differentiated. To follow are examples of experiences that are being transformed by focusing on removing friction and supporting the user's movement or flow.

Open Road Tolling

Toll roads have a surprisingly long history, stretching back at least 2,700 years to the reign of the Assyrian king Ashurbanipal. And for at least 2,680 of those years, toll road users have had to stop and pay at toll gates, stations, booths, or plazas before continuing on their way.

The problems with the pre-tech tolling system are surprisingly long as well. Toll roads can add hours to a commuter's weekly journeys; for example, tolls on Interstate 294 in Illinois added at least two hours per week to the commute (Illinois.gov, 2005). And with the delays come the attendant problems of noise and exhaust pollution. In a 2011 report on congestion in the New York/New Jersey metropolitan area, toll plazas were estimated to be responsible for 40% of the area's total traffic congestion. This translated into 180 million vehicle hours of delay, 140 million gallons of fuel wasted, and $4.36 billion congestion costs, all annually (Ozmen-Ertekin, 2011). On top of that, toll plazas can be dangerous. In 2003 a tractor-trailer plowed into the back of a bus at a tollbooth near Hampshire, Illinois, causing a five-vehicle pileup that claimed eight lives. Subsequently, the National Transportation Safety Board undertook a safety review of tolls and found that they were responsible for 49% of all interstate accidents in Illinois, and that these toll accidents were three times as deadly as other road accidents. Toll plaza accidents also accounted for 38% of all highway accidents on New Jersey toll roads and 30% in Pennsylvania (National Transportation Safety Board, 2005).

In short: not only do crashes cause blockages and stoppages, but blockages and stoppages cause crashes. Any interruption to the flow of traffic can be dangerous, whether by accident or by design.

Fortunately, thanks to a number of technological advances, the stop-and-pay tollbooth model is being superseded by open road tolling (ORT). In the ORT model, cars are identified individually as they drive past (or under) detection points at their normal speed and the car owners are billed accordingly. This can be achieved in various ways and with differing levels of accuracy, completeness, and timeliness. Currently the most effective method for everyone concerned includes a transponder in the car that communicates with an antenna at the detection point (built by default at the site of the former toll booths/plazas). The driver pre-purchases the transponder and an initial monetary balance; then, each time the antenna detects the transponder it debits the toll from the balance.

According to KPMG's Toll Benchmarking Study (2015), toll systems employing the transponder cost the operator between $0.17 and

$0.34 per transaction, whereas the original cash systems cost between $0.72 and $1.00—a difference of one-quarter to one-third.

There is a broader lesson to be learned here, because many of our everyday consumer experiences are designed with the same model of stopping and waiting for service. Checkout lines at grocery stores and other retail outlets, waiting rooms at doctor's offices, telephone-based queues for "the next available agent," check-in lines at hotels—plus the dreaded check-in and security and boarding at airports (three queues in a row!).

This model is clearly easier for the service providers to implement but almost inevitably harder for the customers, whose money is clearly valued more than their time. But as the example of the toll booth shows, making it easy for the provider does not necessarily equate to making it cost-effective for them as well.

Just Walk Out Shopping

If only we could enjoy the benefits of ORT in grocery stores, which across the US receive 30 million shoppers per day (Radic, 2023). And although express lanes are popular, from the retailer's perspective they are not ideal, because nearly one in four customers considers buying fewer items to avoid waiting behind fully loaded shopping carts (King, 2018). Self-checkout lanes are another popular option, but there are lines to use them, too. So some customers take advantage of curbside pickup or simply do their grocery shopping online.

Into this space comes Amazon's Go stores powered by its "Just Walk Out" technology. As of March 2023, there were 29 Amazon Go stores in the US, albeit with plans to close eight of them in April (Riley, 2023), with variants in the UK. As long as customers have the Amazon Go app installed on their smartphones, they can enter the store, do their shopping, and leave—without having to endure any waiting at all. The app is connected to their Amazon account and their purchases are billed to that account automatically. The shopping process is supported by in-store technologies including cameras and other sensors that can tell when items are removed from and replaced to the shelves—and all of these systems are integrated with accounting, inventory management, shopping trends, customer information, and other business intelligence capabilities.

The benefits of this type of technology are wide ranging. The first and foremost is of course the frictionless customer experience, so it is perhaps no surprise that Amazon is at the forefront with its reputation for customer centricity. But the retailer itself also benefits, in several ways. With the integration of back and front office systems, it has much more accurate and timely data and it requires fewer employees—and those employees are freed from the manual and repetitive nature of the checkout process. And because the store itself no longer needs to reserve space for checkout, by some accounts that reduces the real estate needed by up to 12%. And with the checkout gone, the entire design of the space, perhaps including even its parking lots, can be redesigned to better suit the customer experience.

Amazon is not only applying the Just Walk Out technology in their own Go stores, they're making it available to other retailers as well. This is part of a long tradition of Amazon, making the technologies they use (e-commerce, warehousing and logistics, computing capacity, and data storage) available to others, turning what would typically be cost centers into additional revenue generators. Amazon is almost unique in this regard, with this ability to turn their business inside out, exposing what would otherwise be hidden away, profiting from surplus capacity, and always putting the customer's flow (mobility and experience) first.

★ ★ ★

We've deliberately chosen two examples from very different industries and at differing levels of maturity to demonstrate the wide applicability of the Boundless mobility model. When we choose to design experiences to make life easier for the customer, to take stopping and waiting out of the equation and to put flow back in, we are nearly always forced into finding ways that make it better for everyone, including the provider.

And although it's true that the provider may have to improve other parts of its operations in order to make customer-first design possible, the end result can be a win-win, which serves everyone.

Organizations that have designed experiences and solutions following the flow model are typically among the most differentiated and most successful players in their industry or market. In addition to ORT and Amazon.com with its Go store concept are Apple's iPhone (next section), Zappos.com's customer service, Disney's "My Disney Experience" app, and Virginia Mason Medical Center's patient flow system (see Chapter 8). And yet, because these experiences and solutions represent only a small part of the whole, there is still massive opportunity for transformation in this space. Any organization looking for transformative and differentiated success should consider joining the resourceful revolution by designing and implementing flow-based solutions.

Mobile Technology

The launch of Apple's iPhone in June 2007 inaugurated (arguably) the most important product in the history of products—at least in terms of the almost unbelievable breadth and depth of its utility and its equally astonishing reach across the global human population. As of 2022 it was estimated that there were 1.2 billion iPhone users across the world (Wise, 2023). Since its introduction, the iPhone and the entire sub-species of the smartphone it birthed has reached well over half of humanity. By some estimates there are now approximately 6.9 billion smartphone subscriptions worldwide—in a population of 8 billion people (Wise, 2023). That's well over a billion more smartphone users than TV viewers (Wise, 2022)! And we think it's important to emphasize that the smartphone, whether iOS or Android, is first and foremost a tool for individuals—for consumption of media, for enjoyment, for personal use—that connects us all. Smartphones give us our flow as individuals to a degree unprecedented by any other technology, bringing the world to us while we're on the move. A significant and growing percentage of all e-commerce is now performed from mobile devices (Insider Intelligence, 2023)—meaning that, in the near future, companies will need to have fully embraced the mobile-first mindset if they wish to remain competitive.

Another angle on mobile technology concerns the fact that many of us now engage in what we think of as ambient/pervasive/ubiquitous computing. In many cases, the removal of friction from the customer experience and the support of their flow has been made possible by a combination of mobile technology and sensors and smart devices connected via the IoT—all supported by AI for continuous learning and improvement. There has also been significant global efforts to remove friction from the experience of renting cars, scooters, and bikes. And, similar to but preceding Amazon Go, Apple has also done a good job of eliminating the physical checkout register from their stores, enabling their employees to be more dispersed throughout the store to help customers and facilitate their purchasing through mobile devices while freeing up physical space for more products. Disney's MagicBand, launched in 2013, was revolutionary at the time for enhancing the guest experience, facilitating access across the parks and serving up relevant information to users—while also capturing valuable data about their experience to enhance future visits.

One of the big—though not at all sexy—tech problems that still needs to be solved is manual data entry. Any separation between an interaction, for example, a sales professional's call to a customer and the capture of the details of that interaction, wastes time and expertise and can lead to data inaccuracy. We want data to move through the system and through the customer journey, informing each point along the way. Eliminating manual processes such as manual data entry is an essential part of enabling data, and the organization, to move.

At first glance this sounds easy but in practice it's not. We still haven't developed a seamless interface between human conversations, which are flexible in structure and highly fault tolerant (we make inferences about meaning and fill gaps based on real-time context, body language, and other clues, not all verbal), and digital transactions, which are none of those things. Yet combinations of newer technologies that we've already discussed—mobile devices, the IoT, AI with speech recognition, machine learning, and natural language processing—are beginning to come together and will soon create that interface. But to be clear: we're not talking about conversations between humans and devices (for example, Amazon's Alexa, Apple's Siri, or the Google Assistant), although those are important, too. We're talking about human-to-human conversations that a device can listen to, interpret, and capture as meaningful, accurate, real-time data. Once this capability becomes commonplace, not only will the customer experience be improved and the company's data be more complete, more accurate, and more timely but also the employee experience will be significantly improved, in some cases freeing individuals from hours of daily data entry.

Flow at Work

We've already discussed various ways in which the Boundless organization supports and enables its employees, and we've identified the distributed, autonomous workforce as a growing reality of business life. The mobility of the employee is another factor. Employees need to feel that they are able to "move up," that they're not stuck in their current position, and that their employer takes an active role in their progress. This is metaphoric movement.

But they also need to feel able to move freely in the literal sense during the work day. Movement is vital to well-being; it also expands creativity and problem-solving capabilities. And so a Boundless organization will need to consider three interconnected themes in relation to their employees' experience: the design of the workplace itself, the connection to nature, and the role of walking.

> **The design of the workplace.** One of the silo mindsets is that the environment itself—the office, the factory, the store—is regarded purely as the setting within which the action of business takes place. It is assumed to play no part in the work being done or in the efficacy of the individuals and/or teams doing that work. And it is further assumed that the individuals themselves are at their most productive when they are at their seats, in their cubicles, with their heads down. But it is now well established that being physically static, and working in environments that promote being sedentary over being active—so-called "obesogenic" environments—can have significant short- and long-term impact on health, well-being, and productivity (Laskowski, 2022). More and more attention is now being paid to the effect that architecture can have on stimulating or encouraging movement as part of a broader effort to design places that are not only aesthetically pleasing but that also promote feelings of well-being, optimism, curiosity, and connectedness.

> **The connection to nature.** Fortunately, the connection to nature is being promoted within design of the built space. The concepts of biophilia (love of nature) and biomimicry (imitating nature) are becoming increasingly evident in rooftop gardens, "green walls," and other efforts to bring the outside in. This follows studies that have shown that just looking at nature

can be healing (Ulrich, 1984). And the Japanese concept of *Shinrin Yoku*, or forest bathing, has now also been shown to have measurable benefits on psychological well-being (Walton, 2018). Clearly, connection to nature is an essential part of the Boundless mindset.

Walking, well-being, decision-making, and creativity. In an episode of the PBS show *NOVA*, mathematician Andrew Wiles offers the following about his process working on solving Fermat's last theorem, a mathematical claim jotted down by Fermat in the 1630s that had gone unsolved since then:

> When I got stuck and I didn't know what to do next, I would go out for a walk. I'd often walk down by the lake. Walking has a very good effect in that you're in this state of relaxation, but at the same time you're allowing the subconscious to work on you. And often if you have one particular thing buzzing in your mind then you don't need anything to write with or any desk. I'd always have a pencil and paper ready and, if I really had an idea, I'd sit down at a bench and I'd start scribbling away. (*NOVA*, 2000)

Scientists, philosophers, and artists alike across ages and cultures have self-reported the benefits of walking on their powers of creativity and problem-solving. The exact mechanism is not fully understood, but there is no doubt that walking has mental as well as physical benefits.

In short, a truly Boundless mindset embraces this broader sense of movement and the possibility of well-being, problem-solving, and creativity that is made possible through it.

"The most profound technologies are those that disappear."
We opened this chapter with this quote by Mark Weiser (1991), who is considered the "father" of "ubiquitous computing." When we are

successful in making technology "disappear" and we enable our customers to seamlessly carry on in their flow, it can feel to them like, well, nothing! That occurrence results from the removal of most if not all of the previous infrastructure. No more toll plaza. No more checkouts. But, to be beneficial, all movement should be directed and intentional. And, as we'll see in the next chapter on continuity, living systems tend to manage flow as circulatory systems.

8 | Continuity

Process Flow | Circulation |
Mindset and Language

Speed is the new currency of business. You have to be able to respond at the speed of your customer's needs. But you can't be fast if you're not designed to move in the first place. And you can't be designed to move if you prioritize structure and stability over responsiveness and anticipation. To achieve and maintain speed, organizations need to reprioritize and reimagine themselves as continuous flows. This is not obvious and it is not easy. In this chapter we provide real-world examples as well as new models and language to help this reimagining.

Process Flow

In Chapter 7 we discussed the importance and benefits of supporting individuals in their flow and reducing the friction, waiting, and waste associated with common customer experiences. We saw how Open Road Tolling, Amazon Go, and others do this, actualizing three immeasurable benefits: cost savings for themselves, better experiences for their employees, and better experiences for their customers. As we argue in the introduction to this book, despite the very many differences to be found in Boundless companies, they all share this double or triple whammy impact: they and their customers enjoy win–win or non-zero-sum returns.

In this chapter we want to focus on how companies can change their development and production processes in order to be more responsive to customers' ever-increasing and changing demands for their products. We believe that changing these processes to become flow-based rather than batch-oriented not only satisfies current customer demand and anticipates future demand but also reduces costs, cuts waste and waiting, is more responsive to changes in needs, takes up less space, and is often better for the environment too (because of the reduction in waste and failed by-product).

Flow-based processes have their origin in manufacturing. Flow manufacturing emerged in the 1980s from just-in-time and total quality management strategies as an alternative approach to dealing

159

with the challenges faced by all manufacturers: how to satisfy customer demand, reduce costs, and increase efficiency all at the same
time. So we'll briefly explore manufacturing generally before discuss-
ing how flow shows up in other industries.

Manufacturing

Traditional manufacturing strategies have focused on typical
economies-of-scale approaches, as we discussed in Chapter 1. In manufacturing terms this means procurement and production in batch
mode to minimize unit cost and maximize resource productivity. It
also means high inventory levels of raw materials, work in progress,
and finished goods. In times of relatively stable customer demand this
worked, and worked well. But as globalization marched forward, technology kept evolving, and customers started to demand more from
their suppliers: more responsiveness, more innovation, and more cost-
effectiveness—at which point these strategies started to falter. High
inventory levels of unwanted product can be very costly, not just
because of the sunk costs of production but also because of the ongoing cost of defects and obsolescence, physical storage space, and inventory management systems—as well as the ripple-down effects all
through the value chain. And even more important, the cumulative
effects of a batch system make it very difficult to be responsive to
change in customer needs.

By contrast, flow-based companies—Boundless organizations—
start with the customer's needs. Organizationally and culturally, they
are driven by a customer-first mentality that then permeates their
processes and technologies and their products, services, and brands. In
effect, product is "pulled through" the production system by customer demand. In the purest form of flow, nothing gets produced
without first being requested by a customer. This means that there
is no inventory of finished products, no supply without a demand.

And note, this is not about a scarcity mindset or about artificial rarity. This is about reducing waste—in terms of excess inventory, physical space for storage, obsolescence, and post-production defects caused by excessive handling, and improving responsiveness to customer needs.

The product is produced one at a time or as a "one-piece batch." This follows from the first concept and increases speed, because the one piece does not have to wait for other pieces at any stage in the production process before it can move on to the next phase (as it would have in a conventional batch process).

In a flow process there is no waiting or interruption or set-up time between phases. In the ideal flow state, the product is improved or transformed as it moves through the "pipeline." This is not about moving product to different "static" stages where it is improved before moving on again, but about improving it literally as it moves. This approach eliminates the delays caused by the additional inspection and testing of sub-processes required whenever a product crosses boundaries or thresholds into and out of different stages.

The process can be stopped at any time by anyone "on the line" when a problem or defect is either identified or anticipated. In Kaizen terms this is known as *Jidoka*, or automation with a human touch. Stopping a flow process is easier than stopping a batch process because only one piece is at a particular phase at any one time, and so the problems affect only one or a few products. Problem-solving is therefore faster and cheaper, which improves quality on a continuous basis. Because stopping the line always has short-term costs, this calls for "cultural trust" in which there is no blame assigned to the person who stops the line, but rather gratitude offered for that person being engaged enough and caring enough to want to reduce the impact of defects and improve the overall quality going forward. (It should be noted that this is easier said than done. Across all industries, employees "on the line" in companies without a flow culture are often afraid of being blamed for process or equipment failure, and will therefore avoid being the messenger of this information.)

In short, process flow brings greater speed and responsiveness to current and changing customer needs. It creates less waste, fewer defects, and higher quality. It takes up less physical space for production and for the carrying of inventory (raw materials, work in progress, and finished goods). It's cheaper for the producer, it's a more engaging work experience for employees, and, last but by no means least, it creates less environmental impact. Process flow along with experience flow are core components of a Boundless world.

It should be noted that the Toyota Production System (TPS) became—and still is—recognized as the gold standard for managing the manufacturing process. Its focus on customer value and customer pull, a holistic approach to waste elimination, teamwork, and continuous learning and improvement, are instrumental in achieving process flow on a consistent, ongoing basis. It should also be noted that the vast majority of attempts to implement TPS fail. A wide range of success rates has been reported, but there seems to be general consensus that between 60% and 90% of companies fail to implement lean/TPS successfully (Pearce et al., 2018). This is mostly because flow is systemic. It does not work in bits and pieces; it is not siloed. And, as we have discussed throughout the book, it is not the norm. Flow is not obvious in a world designed for structure and control.

Pharmaceuticals

Flow manufacturing has been practiced in some areas of manufacturing for several decades (e.g., automobiles, oil refining, food production, semiconductors). But it is still relatively new in others—including pharmaceutical drug manufacturing. Traditionally, drugs are produced in batch mode by mixing together large volumes of chemicals in industrial vats. *Batch mode* refers not just to the quantities involved but also to the fact that the process is split into a number of different phases, with the entire batch going through one phase before proceeding to the next. Between phases there is always testing required, typically some filtering or purification process, and usually some waiting period. And sometimes the batch needs to be transported from one facility to another between phases.

Continuous or flow manufacturing of drugs happens literally as a flow of chemicals through a reactor or reactors, and all "phases" happen sequentially within the flow. Of course, it's a lot more complex than this description suggests. One pioneer in this realm is Novartis, which entered into a multiyear collaboration with MIT, culminating in the launch of the Novartis Continuous Manufacturing Facility in Basel, Switzerland, in 2017.

Despite the complexity, the benefits of continuous drug manufacturing are expected to be significant, with estimates that manufacturing time could be reduced by up to 90% and costs by 30% to 50% (Fotheringham, 2018). And quality is expected to be improved, because testing can happen mid-flow and the impact of low-quality materials or mistakes in processing can be detected much earlier and will affect a much smaller volume. And wastage will be reduced from excess chemicals and from contamination caused by waiting or by human error. In yet another advantage, continuous drug manufacturing also takes up less physical space than does batch manufacturing.

Perhaps the main driver of flow manufacturing in pharmaceuticals will be in the pursuit of personalized medicine, where medical interventions and therapies are tailored to the individual patient. Although this will take many other factors, including AI, to bring about, it's not likely to be effected via batch processing given both its cost and speed limitations. Flow, however, looks poised to provide a much better alternative, as it does in other parts of Industry 4.0.

Health Care Providers: Virginia Mason Medical System

> *"Many [leaders] in health care are in leadership positions because they are able to do amazing things to save the day—people who can manage in a crisis. But we don't want a crisis. We want systems and standard work to prevent a crisis. Success depends not on the actions of a charismatic, heroic individual, but on the system."*
>
> *—Sarah Patterson, principal executive, Sensei, Virginia Mason Institute (Arthur, 2015)*

The principles of continuous-flow manufacturing are by no means limited to the factory floor or to the manufacturing industries themselves. After experiencing financial losses in 1998 and 1999, Virginia Mason Medical System (VMMS), a health care system based in Seattle, Washington, decided to attack the problem of waste in its own operations and turned to the TPS for guidance. The story goes that a TPS "sensei" (a teacher or someone who has achieved mastery in a particular field, in this case the TPS) reviewed the floorplans of one of the VMMS facilities and asked about the purpose of various spaces. When the hospital team replied they were waiting areas—where patients might wait for up to 45 minutes before being seen—he asked if they were ashamed! Of course, initially they were confused, because waiting rooms are a usual part of every health care facility. But they later realized that waiting is a form of waste and an indication of inefficient processes. And even worse, it is of zero value, perhaps even of negative value, to the patients themselves. And so the VMMS set out to eliminate waiting. They redesigned work spaces and practices, including the real-time handling of documentation rather than batching it, and created a new position: the flow manager. Via their combined efforts they managed to cut out waiting almost completely—which produced an unexpected impact. The medical staff members were able to see at least 20% more patients per day, without either reducing their time with each patient or increasing their hours—which of course increased satisfaction among all involved. And as VMMS continued to apply these principles and practices across more and more of their facilities and departments, they started to see financial benefits as well. They went from losing money to earning positive margins every year. Their liability insurance costs declined by 74%, their operating room throughput increased by 40%, and nurses increased the amount of their time spent with patients from 35% to 90% (Arthur, 2015).

More recently, VMMS have started using AI to help them understand their entire system of care (Jong, 2021). It enables them to provide better care, a better experience, and higher quality by focusing on each individual patient more quickly than they could with just the electronic medical record.

The work will never be finished, of course. VMMS is continually scrutinizing their operations to eliminate waste, improve quality, and increase patient satisfaction. Fortunately, they're also sharing their developments with others: they founded the Virginia Mason Institute (virginiamasoninstitute.org) to spread benefits across the health care ecosystem and beyond.

Retail: Zara, Fast by Design

June 9, 2001. Barcelona, Spain. The opening night of Madonna's Drowned World Tour. Recently married to the film director Guy Ritchie, Madonna and her back-up dancers rocked the first set dressed in bondage gear and tartan, designed by the French designer Jean Paul Gaultier, in apparent homage to her husband's Scottish ancestry.

Just a few nights later, several of the girls in the front rows were wearing kilts that looked just like Madonna's. Except that Gaultier didn't make them. They had been designed, produced, and distributed to stores in just the few days between shows by Zara, the Spanish retail fashion brand ("The Future of Fast Fashion," 2005).

It's hard to exaggerate how radical this speed to market was in the fashion world (which nowadays is roughly a $1.5 trillion global industry; Statista, 2023). The established business model at the time was for retailers to preorder their entire stock for a season from their suppliers six to nine months ahead of time—up to 20 times slower than Zara had. This meant that the whole industry had to forecast, or guess, what styles and colors would be on trend a year or more in advance. Even the greatest instincts can be wrong, of course. In that same year The Gap, the dominant US fashion retailer, tragically mis-forecast trends and was left with billions of dollars' worth of unsold and unwanted inventory that created knock-on effects felt for years afterward.

Speed has continued to be the key to Zara's success. Seven years after the Madonna tour, Zara (or, more accurately, Inditex, its parent company) bested The Gap as the world's largest fashion retailer. Its annual revenues in 2022 were about $19.6 billion. And the company's founder, Amancio Ortega, has become one of the world's wealthiest people, even briefly taking over the top spot as the world's richest man in 2015.

So how is Zara able to perform so fast and maintain its relevance? In a nutshell, it took the industry-standard methodologies and flipped them on their head. Instead of ordering, producing, and shipping large quantities of product once or twice per year, it designs and produces fashion items in small batches that it distributes to its stores worldwide twice a week, often by air despite the higher shipping costs. It uses direct and immediate customer feedback—what they buy, what they try on but leave in the changing rooms, what they say they like and don't like, and so on—to tweak the next iteration of designs (Rohwedder & Johnson, 2008). As Ortega himself has said, "the customer has always driven the business model" (Pattani, 2016). Even a few customer comments can trigger a rapid, global response, as we saw in the story of Zara and the pink scarf in Chapter 3.

Because they produce only small quantities, Zara generates scarcity and demand, minimizes the overhead costs and waste of unsold inventory, and creates safe, low-risk conditions for experimentation. This is made possible via the flow of sales and customer information from the store to the design team, the flow of design specifications from the design team to the production facility, the flow of finished goods from production to the logistics center, and the flow of packaged product from the logistics center to the store. This sequence is circular and continuous, enabling rapid and low-friction responsiveness to the customer and a low-cost approach to managing constant changes in demand. And, in turn, customers visit the Zara stores up to five times more frequently than the industry norm.

Mobility and Continuity

What Zara makes particularly clear is how being built on the principles of mobility and continuity have enabled the company to be so fast—and thus so successful.

The idea that speed is enabled by mobility comes from the basic fact that a body in motion can respond more quickly to a dynamic situation than a body at rest. That's why outfielders in baseball and cricket and defensive backs in football start to move even before the ball is pitched or bowled or snapped. And that's why the first leg of an elite-level 4 × 100 meter relay, which has a standing rather than moving start, typically takes 1 to 1.5 seconds longer than the other three legs (Larsson, 2023). And that's a massive difference, the equivalent of at least 11 meters, in a sport where differences are typically measured in millimeters and hundredths of seconds.

The mobility of information flows from a source (e.g., a complaint from a customer) to the person responsible for acting on it (e.g., an account manager); this person in some way adds value (e.g., an apology, a solution, a gift, etc.), and then the information flows back to the source (the customer), where the response (e.g., an increase in satisfaction or ongoing displeasure) is measured and fed back to improve the process. But in many businesses too often that information is captured but not routed, which means it becomes static, or it's not transformed into value, or the loop is never closed. But mobility can be built and speed can be enabled by paying attention to all the steps in marketing, sales, service, and other core processes and ensuring that value is always flowing through them back to the customer—without being stopped or diverted. That same need for mobility applies equally to information, product, money, expertise, raw material, and other types of resources. And it applies to all companies in all industries as much as it does to natural systems—such as in animals, where blockages and cessations of airflow or blood flow are the leading causes or determinants of death.

Continuity means that this flow is ongoing, not just a single event. A Zara retail store, wherever it is in the world, receives two shipments each week that include small batches of new product items. Continuity means taking a process or event that typically happens only once per year or per season and that generates a single "big" deliverable—and breaking it down into multiple smaller processes that happen frequently and generate multiple smaller deliverables. For example, seasonal inventory ordering that delivers a single large shipment of product can be replaced with a Zara equivalent schedule or a just-in-time inventory system. An annual plan that includes all departmental strategies and budgets for the entire year can be replaced with a rolling plan. An IT strategy that delivers a fully functional system after two years can be replaced with an Agile system development approach that delivers value incrementally and responsively.

In general, continuity-focused companies like Zara favor the many, the small, and the frequent (Zara produces over five times the average number of product lines and manages twice-weekly product shipments in small batches to its stores worldwide) over the industry standard of the few, the large, and the rare.

These same principles apply not just to sustaining life in natural systems and individual business organizations but also to global systems. Two of the (arguably) most important inventions of the 20th century were containerized shipping and the internet. Similar to the circulatory system for the body, they both enable the continuous flow of resources around the world. In the case of containerization, those resources can be anything physical, from fruits and vegetables to cars, equipment, household appliances, fashion items, and so on. And in the case of the internet, they can be any type of digital content.

Agile and DevOps

Continuity has been an important principle in computing ever since the advent of multiuser systems in the 1960s. Since then we have seen shifts from a few centralized mainframes to billions of distributed computing devices, from nightly batch windows to 24/7 online availability, from hierarchical to relational to cloud-based SQL/NoSQL data, from proprietary to open systems, from "monolithic" applications to microservices and APIs, and, potentially, from corporate ownership of customer data to individual ownership by means of the distributed web (as previously mentioned, a current initiative led by Sir Tim Berners-Lee, the "father" of the world wide web). In each case we see the evolution from systems and processes that are centralized and batched to those that are decentralized and in real time.

This same principle applies to digital product or software development and operations, where we are seeing a migration from waterfall methodologies and episodic deployments to Agile and DevOps. Agile prioritizes flow or sprint-based development of software over batch processing, and DevOps aims for continuous testing, integration, delivery/deployment, and monitoring of that software. In truth, Agile is as much or more about people and ways of working as it is about technology. It aims to flatten hierarchies, enable teams to be self-organizing and self-governing, reduce or eliminate bureaucracy—including excessive and static documentation—and improve customer satisfaction by increasing speed to value. In practice, Agile is most effective in situations and organizations that already have cultures of cross-functional communication and non-siloed, timely decision-making. Without this, Agile can get stuck inside broader "waterfall" business processes and lose its intended effect. Nevertheless, Agile, DevOps, and their evolutions represent the future of digital product development in a Boundless world.

Beyond Development and Production

We have focused on continuity in terms of development and production processes both in the physical and digital realms. But as we have hinted in our brief discussion of Agile practices, in order to be continuous as a business—to be organized on the continuous creation and transformation of value—these development and production processes cannot operate effectively within an otherwise siloed organization. The mindset of continuity has to permeate throughout the company. We are beginning to see signs of this happening; for example, groups outside IT and engineering are beginning to use daily stand-ups to communicate more effectively. Agile has been applied to marketing and, to a lesser extent, selling. Rolling budgets and forecasts appear in some finance and accounting departments. *Everboarding* is a comparatively new term, described in 2021 as "cutting edge," for continuous onboarding and learning. These are all good signs—but, where they are practiced in isolation from other core business processes, when they are not part of a continuous mindset, they will soon lose their effectiveness; to succeed, flow needs to be systemic. It is to this mindset that we now turn.

The Continuous Mindset

As we stated at the beginning of this chapter, speed is the new currency of business, meaning the ability of any organization to respond to customer's stated needs, learn their unmet needs, and anticipate their future needs on *their* timeline, not the organization's timeline. Speed itself is impossible without processes and organizational structures that are specifically and intentionally designed to enable the flow, or continuous movement, of information and other valuable resources like product and money.

The challenge is that most companies are simply not designed or governed in that way, and so attempts to move at speed nearly always require a superhuman effort from the most committed employees that is unsustainable and nearly always leads to frustration and often to burnout. Instead, ubiquitous companies across organizations and industries are organized to facilitate the management and control of those same resources through features such as stage-gate processes, decision/approval hierarchies, and departmental silos. Even the directive from leadership for growth seems to prioritize size over speed. All of this is why any company designed for movement—in any line of business or sector or industry—is worth studying. And this is why it's also worthwhile to look beyond business for ideas, examples, and analogies. In this section we briefly consider other ways of thinking about business: from a living-systems perspective and from a language perspective.

Living Systems and Circulation

The silo mindset is focused on accumulation and control—collecting, storing, and classifying resources in the hope that they will generate value at some stage in the future. It leads to keeping a tight grip on annual budgets and plans in the finance department, protecting IP and the brand in the legal department, controlling communications on a need-to-know basis, attracting and "retaining" talent in HR, attracting and "retaining" valued customers in marketing, amassing as much data as possible in IT, and so on. Everywhere we look, the goal of corporate departments, explicitly stated or implicitly understood, is to collect, protect, and control their resources and, if possible, to increase their number.

But this level of resource control and protection can endanger companies' longevity. Fortunately, changing the management paradigm from accumulation and control to movement and sharing—that is, flow—may reverse that trend. It turns out that living systems offer an alternative model to the silo mindset.

We like to talk about key resources as our companies' lifeblood, the most important thing we need to survive or to be successful, and yet we pay no attention to their movement. But if our bodies decided to try out our corporate model of resource management, and our hearts started to store blood instead of pumping it to where it is needed (which just happens to be nearly everywhere in the body), and our lungs started to hold their breath instead of continually bringing in fresh resources from the outside and sharing them with the blood, we would die immediately.

Blood by itself does not ensure life. It's the movement, the flow of the blood delivering nutrients to the body and extracting waste and other harmful products from it that counts. We're dependent on this flow, enabled by the circulatory system, just as we are dependent on the continuous act of breathing enabled by the respiratory system.

This doesn't just apply to humans or animals. Trees also move resources throughout their bodies, from leaves to roots and back via their own circulatory systems. And, as mentioned in Chapter 3, they even exchange information with each other via the recently discovered "wood wide web," also known as a mycorrhizal fungal network (Popkin, 2019). And they exchange resources with us, most notably carbon dioxide and oxygen by way of photosynthesis, arguably the most important process in nature. And although individual trees may not move, forests can. Peter Wohlleben in his marvelous book *The Hidden Life of Trees* estimates that the beech trees of central Europe are migrating northward a quarter mile per year (Wohlleben, 2016).

Flow Components

Aside from blood, there are four key components of the flow paradigm:

Pumps. In organizations, departments become pumps when they prioritize ensuring that essential resources are continuously distributed throughout the organization where they're needed. In a flow-based system, the relationships between departments are more important in a flow-based system than are the departments themselves.

A circulatory system. The flow of resources must be directed and channeled to ensure they get where they're most needed with minimal loss. This means cocreating organization-wide processes for sharing and developing resources. When feedback is built into the system, the pump or originating department knows how and when to accelerate or amplify its efforts—just as the heart and lungs do during physical exertion.

Filters. Organizations need ways to extract from their flows resources that are no longer viable. This may include unworkable ideas, projects that are going nowhere, people who are being counterproductive, and so on. Traditional business pipeline management practices intentionally stop projects in their tracks so their continued usefulness can be decided on. Pumping systems, however, use filters to remove unwanted elements while allowing valued resources to continue unimpeded.

An enriched environment. Organizations, similar to bodies, need a constant or near constant renewal of their energy sources from the outside. This may include income, new information, customers, talent, equipment and tools, innovation and new ideas, raw materials, and so on. Storage of resources can lead to fat, lack of agility, and diminished performance, whereas on-demand exchanges can increase agility and efficiency, as well as reduce waste.

Of course, transforming a silo mindset into a flow mindset is not an easy reframe or paradigm shift. Many of us measure success by the number of resources under our management. But in this emerging world of connectedness, of positive returns and non-zero-sum games, the flow of resources and value among people, departments, and organizations is increasingly valued. Once blockages, accidental or intentional, are removed, resources can flow again—and companies, similar to rivers or bodies or experiences, can come back to life.

Business Continuity Is Life

This is not just metaphorical. Without continuity—when we're able to run our core processes or access our data or use our systems to make sound and timely decisions—our businesses can be seriously compromised or worse. Just as movement is life for individuals, continuity is life for organizations.

For this reason, companies that provide solutions or services that form some critical part of their customers' operations need to consistently maintain their customers' continuity as well—and before those customers even know there is a problem. These businesses need to behave like autonomous technologies that can self-detect and self-repair, and to proactively make use of those technologies—primarily IoT-connected and intelligent devices—to sense actual or probable failure with the solution or service and to repair it before the customer is even aware of it. Detecting and correcting, predicting and preventing are the keys to ensuring that customers can continue to run their business operations without interruption.

The Language of Continuity

Companies are not things; they are neither static objects nor physical entities. And yet we often conceptualize our organizations as structures, specifically, architectural structures. And to keep these structures stable, they have to be firmly established. Surveys need to be made, trenches have to be dug, concrete has to be poured. Only when our foundation is in place can we build on it. Foundations provide the stability needed to resist the elements. Whether we fear the big bad wolf or market volatility, we need a strong foundation to prevent our house from being blown down.

Similarly, organizations pictured within this architectural mindset might be imagined like a Greco-Roman temple, with the pillars being our values, each value a building block. The same ideas are behind models of modern platforms and protocols, with foundational technologies—those that change least and that other capabilities are built on—on the base. Platforms, from oil rigs to operating systems, distance us from the turmoil below and undergird other capabilities above. Protocol stacks are envisaged in the same way.

Although platforms themselves are vital, we need to rethink our mental model. We need to consider an entire company as a platform— but one not built to resist change but to lean into change. In the old model, stability protects our resources; in this new era, stability retards responsiveness. The platform of tomorrow enables maneuverability, taking advantage of emerging technologies such as AI that enable us to "fly by wire."

As we have argued in Chapters 3 and 5, the seemingly paradoxical idea that we should embrace instability is much easier to grasp when

we also have the worldview that companies are processes, not structures. This new worldview needs to be accompanied and supported
by a new language, by new metaphors. In addition to "living systems"
and "circulation" and "pumps," if we want to design processes rather
than structures, we'll want to apply more verbs to our thinking.

Question: *When is an owl not an owl?*
Answer: *When it is a "perches on the lower branches of the spruce tree."*

To the Koyukon people of northern Alaska, animals *are* what they
do, and they name them accordingly, using verbs that describe their
activities and behavior (perching) rather than nouns that classify them
(boreal owl). The Koyukon have been mostly nomadic for a thousand
years, following the herds, and their animal names reflect a belief in life
as movement (Ingold, 2011). On the other side of the planet, and in a
very different climate, the Australian Aboriginals also experience life as
movement, as is expressed in their art, their rites of passage, and their
origin myths—as well as in their traditional daily mode of existence.

Thinking more in verbs could enable us to apply an entirely new
lens to our world today—and perhaps make it easier to imagine and
assimilate a Boundless future.

9 | Shared Success

Experiences | Technologies | Business Models

> "*There is symbiosis at every single level of living things, and you cannot compete in a zero-sum game with creatures upon whom your existence depends.*"
>
> —*Richard Powers (2020)*

We opened the introduction of this book with a discussion of Chef José Andrés and his crisis-relief organization, World Central Kitchen (WCK). We started there because he so neatly encapsulates the Boundless mindset and the kind of value outcomes that all leaders and all organizations, regardless of industry and classification, can achieve when they design themselves and their offerings on the Boundless principles we have laid out across Chapters 3–8.

Chef Andrés has shown us that there is a model for providing relief that operates on a different premise to the conventional one. The premise is not about the efficient use of an organization's own resources, maximizing output and minimizing unit cost. It is about the effective use of an ecosystem's resources, maximizing value for all of its members. It scales differently, with greater flexibility and adaptability, and can work alongside the traditional model in some cases and perhaps even replace it in others.

Production is decentralized and distributed, marshaling community-based resources—namely, local restaurants—with their existing infrastructures built specifically to serve and feed the local community. It can be scaled up and, crucially, scaled down as needed without significant cost or effort—simply by inviting more restaurants, their teams, and their equipment into the initiative. This minimizes or negates the need for investment in centralized infrastructure, which would be built for exceptional and, ideally, rare circumstances.

And, even more important, this new model engages more people and creates a virtuous cycle where everyone who is part of it becomes part of the value flow. In the old model the service provider takes a linear, direct approach to problem-solving—people are hungry, we will feed them—that is set up and runs separately from existing solutions instead of connecting and integrating with them. In the new ecosystem model, more people are connected and enjoy reciprocal benefits:

WCK itself as the service provider benefits from knowing people will get hot, good-quality meals, from being able to scale without having to invest in infrastructure, and without having to supervise and control any of the meal production processes.

Restaurant owners benefit from being able to keep their businesses going, their staff members working and paid. And $135 million has gone from donors, via WCK, to restaurants (Mandelbaum, 2020).

Restaurant workers benefit from getting paid to do what they're good at and being able to serve community members in need. They are able to support themselves and their families and to spend money on other services that they value and therefore keep other people employed as well.

Donors benefit from knowing that their contributions not only provide nutritious and delicious food to those in need but also supports local businesses and workers. WCK started the initiative with $10 million but was (Mandelbaum, 2020) "buoyed by a surge of donations, much of it in small contributions" totaling about $150 million.

Volunteers no longer engage at the point of production, where cooking skills are most valuable but rather at the point of exchange of the meals to the hungry, where human empathy and compassion are the most important skills.

The hungry benefit from the emotional and psychological comfort and pleasure that comes from a well-cooked, quality meal, not just having their functional needs satisfied.

We call this a model of shared success. It's a non-zero-sum game, and has hints of what Robin Wall Kimmerer calls the gift economy (Kimmerer, 2022), which is based on the principles of gratitude and reciprocity. At its most actionable, shared success for companies comes from putting the success of their employees, customers, ecosystem partners, and communities on an equal footing with their own financial success. As we previously noted in Chapter 5, research has demonstrated the direct link among employee engagement, customer engagement, and growth. Similarly we have also shown that companies that focus on the success of their business ecosystems are rewarded in turn by those ecosystems. And according to a Deloitte study, "Purpose-driven companies witness higher market share gains and grow three times faster on average than their competitors, all while achieving higher workforce and customer satisfaction" (O'Brien et al., 2019).

Shared success can, therefore, be a defining principle not just for innovative humanitarian organizations such as WCK but for all companies who want to be successful in the emerging digital-first, individual-first world. And this isn't a lofty ideal that is unattainable for all but the most specialized or niche organizations. All of the companies, processes, and experiences that we have showcased in this book are leading practitioners and practices in their industries.

To be clear, we are not saying that companies need to ditch profit to be successful. And we are not saying that the only "good" companies are nonprofit organizations like WCK. We're not saying that you need to be a visionary like Yvon Chouinard at Patagonia, who has set the standard for responsible production while building a loyal customer base and growing a profitable business over the last half century. What we are saying is that if you design for flow and connectedness and if you take care and respect all the resources at your disposal, human and otherwise, and if you organize for these same things, then you'll achieve the kinds of results that we've featured here. You'll become responsive, and you'll become that way not because of the heroism of a few key people but because of the effectiveness of your systems, human, digital, and hybrid. Your own success will increase, not diminish.

The key to your success though is not to start with it. It's to start with your customer's success: how do you deliver the greatest possible value to them and create the least possible friction doing so? And how do you provide the most engaging experience for your own people to motivate them to deliver that value on a continuous basis? And how do you engage with other members of the ecosystem to accelerate and amplify that value? Once you've organized your processes and systems and people around that, your own success will follow.

So let's briefly revisit some of the examples we have provided along the way and introduce others to show how shared success is a guiding principle and a quantifiable outcome of becoming Boundless.

Boundless Experiences

We are all familiar with experiences in our daily lives that force us to stop in our tracks and thus take us out of our flow. In Chapter 7 we described how the toll plaza experience has been transformed thanks to open road tolling (ORT), which provides a vastly superior motorist experience. No stopping, no wasting time in rush hour lines, no searching for exact change, no getting stuck behind "that" driver—and no getting struck by the driver behind you. Instead, ORT is designed specifically to enable you to continue your journey without interruption or frustration—in essence to maintain your flow. It's also cheaper for everyone whose time equals money, including commuters, taxi drivers, and truckers. And the municipality collecting the tolls benefits, too; ORT is cheaper to manage and maintain than the cash-based toll booths, and its continuous stream of data may prove to be useful in a variety of ways, for instance, in providing accurate traffic density and flow figures, helping to manage peak densities in and out of cities, and enabling accurate revenue calculations. And because

ORT eliminates stopping and waiting, it also increases fuel efficiency and reduces carbon monoxide and other emissions, providing an environmental benefit as well.

Another example of a flow-based or Boundless experience—one still in its early days but which will inevitably evolve to take share from its current silo counterpart—is checkout-free retail, currently being led by Amazon Go and already followed by several others. In many respects, checkout-free retail is nearly identical to ORT in its benefits, saving the customer time and irritation, improving the retailer's data capture, while saving employment costs and improving the use of space (an environmental benefit). And it is also enabled by a similar, distributed technology model, with mobile technology at the customer end (smartphone for retail, transponder for ORT) and sensing technology at the retailer end. Distributing intelligence to the customer and provider is a profound facilitator of the Boundless model in general, already enabling experiential innovations in a range of industries.

Boundless Technologies

In only 15 or so years since its introduction to the world, Apple's iPhone and the entire sub-species of mobile smartphones that it has birthed has achieved quite extraordinary reach and impact. It has reached at least two-thirds of all humanity in that short time. Smartphones give us our flow as individuals to a degree unprecedented by any other technology. Not only does it untether us from the landline but also it brings the world to us while we are on the move. A significant and growing percentage of all e-commerce is now performed from mobile devices and in the near future companies will need to have fully embraced the mobile-first mindset that has been percolating for the last decade or so. The smartphone has also created an entirely new ecosystem of apps developers and accessory producers, and, of course, Apple itself and its competitors have benefited immensely from their inventions. The iPhone accounts for some 50% of the company's annual revenues compared to the Mac, the company's "legacy" product, at approximately 10%.

The autonomous car is an obvious example of mobility because it moves, but there is far more to this evolving technology. Autonomy actually requires that the car is far more connected to its world than it has ever been, it needs to be sensing everything that's going on around it continuously, it needs to decide what it needs to do and then it needs to respond to those external conditions. And it delivers benefits to the human, who is free to do what they want as a traveler rather than as a machine operator. It can be mobile continuously serving multiple human needs rather than being parked in a garage or on the side of the street for most of the time, and it will be much safer given that more than 90% of all car crashes are the result of human behaviors and emotions. Although full autonomy seems further off than anticipated, it can only be a matter of time before it is achieved and at that point it won't only save the manufacturers money, it will become their dominant revenue stream.

Boundless Business Models

To follow we share examples of how Boundless business models have affected numerous industries.

Enterprise software. Salesforce delivers three major releases annually to its CRM product, predictably and reliably. They have achieved this by adopting Agile practices and philosophy, enabling the flow of information among customers, salespeople, partners, developers, and others. They also designed and implemented a process for developing annual goals and gaining organizational alignment on them from the earliest days of the company. Known as the V2MOM for vision, values, methods, obstacles and measures, the entire company is engaged in its development in one way or another and everyone can see everyone else's individual version, enabling a flow of information from top to bottom and across the entire organization that is second to none. Salesforce has a strong commitment to its ecosystem of developers, admins, and architects, all of whom benefit from building skills and experience and careers on the platform, and through its programs such as its 1:1:1 philanthropic model—1% product, 1% time, 1% profit donated—the company is also able to provide its world-class platform to organizations who wouldn't otherwise be able to afford it.

Retail. The Spanish fashion retail chain Zara (which we first discussed in Chapter 3) is built on a continuous flow and feedback model. They produce and distribute in small batches, reducing the design-to-shelf cycle time from an industry average of six to nine months to two to four weeks. They maintain low inventory levels in their stores. Information flows daily from consumers to designers—what they say they'd like to see, what they try on but discard in the dressing room, and what they actually buy—and responsive product flows back to them. The designers review all this data every morning and shape their decisions and designs based on this and other feedback. And it works. Their parent company, Inditex, took over from The Gap as the largest retail fashion company in the world in 2008, and its founder is one of the world's richest people.

Energy and industry. The Danish eco-industrial park of Kalundborg (discussed in Chapters 3 and 5) stands alone in its commitment to industrial symbiosis, the sharing between organizations of by-products as resources, including energy and material, to reduce waste, costs, and environmental pollution.

Since its initial experiments in 1972 membership has grown to
include over 30 by-product exchange agreements between
some of Denmark's largest organizations. Between them they
have reduced yearly CO_2 emission by 240,000 tons, saved 3 million cubic meters of water through recycling and reuse, and
recycled 150,000 tons of gypsum. The park as a whole operates
as a flow system, providing inspiration, example, and analogy for
innovative multi-organizational collaborations of all types.

Public education. High Tech High (HTH) School in San
Diego, California, rejects most educational norms. It removes
the distinctions between school and community, adult and student, academic and technical, privileged and underprivileged,
and draws connections between them all through field studies,
community service, internships, consultation with industry
partners, and other outside experts, and exhibitions in professional venues. Some 98% of HTH graduates go on to post-
secondary education compared to a national average of
approximately 66%. As a result, it has ranked as high as the
number 1 STEM school in the USA (science, technology,
engineering, and mathematics) by *U.S. News & World Report*.

Health care. Virginia Mason Medical Center turned around a
series of financial losses by studying and applying principles
from the Toyota Production System and in particular by focusing on the customer/patient experience. By recognizing waiting as a form of waste and setting out to eliminate it from as
many parts of its operations as possible, it has managed to
improve patient satisfaction as well as nurse satisfaction, has
increased the number of patients that the doctors can consult
and treat without increasing their hours, and has increased
revenues and delivered positive margins ever since. It has also
developed Virginia Mason Institute in order to enable others

to learn from their experience and build flow into their operations and achieve similar beneficial outcomes for everyone involved.

Memorial Sloan-Kettering reimagined chemotherapy treatment from the bottom up and from the patient's perspective, starting with the insight that time, especially time spent with family, is their patients' most valuable and precious commodity. At the Brooklyn Infusion Center, waiting times have been eliminated. Patients are free to move around, bring family members with them, and create a soothing or healing environment for themselves. The work flow is so different from the norm that nurses are cross-trained as Reiki massage therapists and can provide guided imagery and other integrative therapies as their patients receive their infusions. All at high safety and quality levels and at a lower cost than the traditional model.

Agriculture. The Spanish fish farm Veta La Palma (which we first discussed in Chapter 2) has turned the traditional agricultural model on its head. To recap: Veta La Palma doesn't isolate its animals from other parts of the ecosystem—it allows them to integrate fully. It doesn't feed its animals—it allows them to feed from their ecosystem, as they would in the wild. It doesn't kill its predators—it measures the success of the farm by their well-being. It does not pollute or impoverish the environment—it actually purifies and enriches it. It has become a bird and wildlife sanctuary, and it provides direct income to about 100 people from the neighboring villages.

In fact, all successful regenerative farms, both land and ocean based, achieve the same non-zero-sum results. Pioneers such as White Oak Pastures have also demonstrated the ability of regenerative farms to revitalize rural communities. And although there are undoubtedly organizations that use the term *regenerative* as mere greenwashing, there are emerging standards and classifications that elevate the success of the farm's natural and human resources as core requirements. The Regenerative Organic Classified (ROC) designation is based not only on meeting current standards for organic agriculture but also on a framework that includes guidelines for soil health and land management, animal welfare, and farmer and worker fairness. Tablas Creek in Paso Robles, California, is the world's first vineyard to achieve the ROC designation. It had already attained organic and biodynamic status but to become regenerative it not only had to care for the land, its vines, and animals but also had to focus on its workers' well-being as well. Quite apart from the resultant improvements in job satisfaction, managers found that the workers were more likely to report problems with equipment before those problems turned into failures and reduce costs of maintenance and replacement. Although in a very different industry this bears strong similarities to the Andon system in manufacturing, empowering any employee to stop the production line should they observe or even suspect a quality issue. Finally, Tablas Creek, through its regular communications and its differentiated, high-quality product, is able to sell its wines directly to consumers through its wine clubs and online store, reducing its costs of sales and improving its margins.

WCK knows already that the same model won't work in all situations. It has responded to other crises where local restaurants were themselves knocked out, meaning that something more akin to the traditional "commissary" needed to be set up. But this adaptability is a key to sustained innovation and growth. Success comes not from depending on a particular innovative solution that worked in the past but rather from depending on the spirit of situational awareness and timely responsiveness that generated the solution in the first place. And even greater success comes from designing for the success of others in the ecosystem, knowing that the greater the resilience of the ecosystem the greater the resilience of the individual members of it, and vice versa.

10

Becoming Boundless

Mindset | Operating Model | Relationships

Boundless companies transcend the limits of traditional organizations. They are designed to achieve shared success, generating value for their customers, business partners, and communities, as well as for themselves and their employees. This success is realized by resources that are individually empowered to be autonomous, connected, and mobile, and that are collectively organized to be integrated, distributed, and continuous.

It's natural to ask where to start on the road to becoming Boundless. Well, it depends. But there are some points we can offer to get you started on a successful path:

- First, the Boundless model is so different (and not in any way obvious) that the normal rules of business just don't apply. Boundless is a new way of organizing and operating that redefines success from a profit-first perspective to a holistic one— where profit, purpose, and value are mutually reinforcing, not mutually exclusive. To succeed in this journey, leaders would be wise to fully assimilate the Boundless **principles** and the ways of thinking that come with them. They need to try on not only the Boundless mindset but also the new metaphors and language that come with it. (We will briefly review the principles following.)
- Second, pursuing Boundlessness calls for reimagining an organization's **operating model**, especially in how it enables the business to be in a state of constant flow and connectedness. The operating model reflects the idea of the company being more like a modern technological system: technological, but also living. (We will reflect and expand on our previous discussion of the autonomous operating model following.) The Boundless operating model supports and enables continuity and enables the organization to focus on reducing waste of all types.

- Third, pursuing Boundlessness calls for (re)designing **core business processes** so that they begin from the perspective and goal of **customer value** and success. All processes need to reflect the Boundless operating model and enable and support flow, taking inspiration from the examples that we shared in Chapters 7 and 8. Doing this will enable cost reduction (by eliminating waste), increased responsiveness to changing customer needs, and improved quality. As you no doubt gleaned long ago, this is not a one-and-done undertaking. All of the examples provided in this book are ongoing and require a mindset of continuous learning, improvement, and innovation.

- Fourth, pursuing Boundlessness calls for developing a **relationship strategy** to (1) define the kinds of relationships you want to have with your customers and (2) to define what other relationships are important to you, including (as relevant) business ecosystems, communities, and the environment. Relationship strategy and its accompanying design capability—relationship design—are big topics in their own right—too much to cover in this book—but we will briefly define the key characteristics or components of a successful relationship to get you started thinking about what you'd like the future of your business relationships to look like.

In this chapter we will recap the Boundless principles, discuss its operating model, and introduce the components of successful business relationships. After that we'll introduce a few final considerations for planning a Boundless journey.

Leadership Mindset

The Boundless model is first and foremost a new mindset for business leaders and designers to remain relevant and achieve success in this changing world. Each of the principles that we've discussed at length in the preceding chapters is a way of thinking and a way of working. So here let's briefly recap each one. All organizations on the journey toward becoming Boundless—regardless of industry, region, or size—share most or all of these design principles:

Organizations on the journey toward becoming Boundless **connect** to the outside world more deeply than their silo counterparts do. They are connected to their partner ecosystems, customers, and communities. At the simplest level they deeply listen to their customers and readily respond to them. At the most complex level they work hand in hand with local businesses and other community partners, extending their reach through empowering others.

Organizations on the journey toward becoming Boundless are **distributed** or decentralized, meaning that they serve their customers and communities locally rather than requiring their customers to come to them. They are equipped and organized to enable working from anywhere, and they are ready to exploit current and future waves of technologies that extend their reach outward.

Internally, the systems of organizations on the journey toward becoming Boundless are **integrated** to (1) enable sharing of data and other resources across the organization and (2) support end-to-end customer journeys and relationships. Their employees are all aligned on their core purpose, vision, and values—which keep them working toward the same goals even when they're working from anywhere.

Organizations on the journey toward becoming Boundless believe in **autonomy** so that their employees feel they have agency and meaning in their work, their customers feel empowered, and their communities become self-sufficient and resilient. They embrace AI, machine learning, and autonomy and other technologies that become *partners* in their work and missions, not just tools.

Organizations on the journey toward becoming Boundless design for **movement** and mobility, literally and figuratively. Their workplaces are designed to promote movement; their business processes ensure that data, product, and decision-making all flow; their employees are encouraged and enabled to move physically for health and to have mobility in their careers. Organizations enable mobility for their customers as well, ensuring that they can be supported wherever they are; and they drive core business communications and processes through mobile technologies by default.

Organizations on the journey toward becoming Boundless practice **continuity** in their processes. They introduce improvements and innovations to the business on a frequent basis. They make decisions quickly to enable teams and initiatives to flow more smoothly. They apply Agile techniques to their digital processes, and they apply analogous practices to other processes, including sales, marketing, finance, and others. Through continuity they are set up for speed when speed is necessary, and for responsiveness more broadly.

And, last but by no means least, organizations on the journey toward becoming Boundless are driven in all decisions, processes, and experiences to enable **shared success.** Profit is important to them because it enables them to keep delivering value and having positive impact—but they design for customer, employee, partner, community, and environment success *first*, and they enjoy the benefits of doing so. They believe in win–win–win effects or non–zero-sum games.

In this book we've used examples from a broad spectrum to show that Boundless is truly Boundless in the sense that it can be applied to any industry in any region. And though we hardly touched on the field of education, note that there too we've seen recent moves toward lifelong learning, self-organized learning environments, badges and micro-certifications and credentials, forest schools, and many other nontraditional, online and hybrid learning experiences that challenge the concept that the only education that counts happens in schools to children separate from and before adult working life. We didn't touch on the penal system at all, but there we see a significant physical and philosophical difference between the traditional prison system (that literally isolates and immobilizes prisoners) and other systems—like Halden, the Norwegian prison designed to facilitate the reintegration of offenders back into society on the completion of their sentence. And we haven't discussed urban and "metroburban" planning, where we see more live-work-play, mixed-use developments—like New Jersey's Bell Works, which integrates rather than segregates different aspects of the lives of its residents. Indeed, wherever we look, we see evidence of a Boundless mindset offering an effective alternative to the silo mentality.

Again, we encourage leaders to think deeply about how these principles apply to them and to their business. At the risk of overstating the case, Boundless organizations are among the most successful in their industries—and their success comes *with* the success of their customers and partners and others, not *at* their expense.

Metaphors and Language

As leaders and designers adopt the Boundless mindset, they will also want to adopt new metaphors and new language. The most important language change comes with the principles themselves.

The principles of mobility and continuity give us opportunities to rethink our most basic assumptions and ideas about how we organize to do business. Do we organize as *structures*, with expectations and norms for nouns and entities, structural stability, resistance to change, identity and the difference between insiders and outsiders, resource acquisition and retention? Or do we organize as *processes*, with a new set of expectations for verbs and relationships, resource flow, inherent plasticity, and responsiveness, "blurred" or collective identity, and the connectedness among organizations, ecosystems, communities, and the environment?

If we choose the latter, then we need to use the language of flow-based and circulatory systems. We need to talk about pumps that enable our resources to be replenished or enriched before being delivered to the parts of those systems that need them most, that enable us to be responsive to the changing needs of customers without requiring superhuman or heroic efforts. Our departments become pumps, and we recognize that the relationship between departments is more important than the departments themselves. The real-time flow of data becomes possible in a process organization as well as the continuous improvement of our algorithms and decision-making as a result of that flow. Our organizations start to come alive when our resources flow.

The principles of connection and autonomy enable us to think about our relationships, internally and externally. They challenge us to consider our connections, to the broader business world and to our relationships with our customers. We no longer regard our businesses as centers or try to put our customers there. Instead we turn our focus outward to where our customers really are and where they're trying to go and we develop our relationships with them based on that and based on mutual value.

These principles even enable us to reconsider our relationships with the world. Indigenous peoples have always contended that we are deeply connected to nature, that we are actually part of it, and this heightened sense of connection brings with it a sense of responsibility and also the opportunity for reciprocity. We have seen that using natural resources doesn't have to mean the same as exploitation. We can give back and in doing so can even increase the world's well-being and carrying capacity.

At the same time these principles also give us a new operating model that is based on emerging technological systems. In order to help leaders and designers apply the principles and metaphors and language of Boundlessness, let's briefly describe that model.

The Boundless Operating Model

The traditional operating model is based on the idea that a company is a thing, an entity, a structure. But Boundless organizations are differentiated in their responsiveness to current and future customer needs and market conditions and in their associated decision-making and action taking. We introduce the Boundless operating model, our update to other contemporary sense-and-respond or situational awareness models, as a guide to help organizations design and develop the necessary processes and capabilities for amplifying and accelerating their responsiveness.

How do companies make themselves aware of what's going on around them, and how do they respond to those inputs? As we started to think about how companies can develop these capabilities, we looked at other situational awareness models to see what we could learn from them. One of the models that we have used is known as the observe-orient-decide-act loop, aka the OODA loop, that was designed by military strategist John Boyd. His goal was to explain how fighter pilots can excel in a combat setting. His insight was that the ability to sense and respond to rapidly changing conditions more quickly than an adversary gives the pilot a competitive advantage. The OODA loop describes the processes required to sense and respond and enables the military to design the most streamlined ways of doing so. This model has been broadly adopted by the military and by businesses who can use it as a conceptual framework for designing and developing business management processes. The goal, as in the military setting, is to enable faster strategic decision-making and innovating than competitors through effective process management.

As we did our research, we realized that the OODA loop is very similar to the sense-perceive-decide-actuate model that is used to describe how autonomous vehicles work. In this model, the vehicle performs the following functions in real time and continuously:

Sense. The vehicle uses its sensors to gather real-time data about its immediate environment or situation—primarily the road and nearby vehicles. *Sense* is a broader word than *observe*, and reflects (1) the fact that not all sensors are based on sight and (2) that they're not assessing the meaning of the data they're gathering and sharing.

Perceive. The vehicle interprets the data that the sensors are sharing and makes sense of them, using machine learning and AI to do so. As we discussed in Chapter 6, Tesla has developed its own supercomputer, Dojo, to train the on-vehicle intelligence with data from across its fleet to improve the accuracy of its perception and decision-making.

Decide. The vehicle then selects from among the options available to it and decides on the safest course of action, again using its AI to do so.

Actuate. The vehicle initiates the actions that it has decided to take. The three primary controls that an autonomous car needs to actuate are the throttle for acceleration, the steering for direction, and the brake for stopping. Of course there are many other actuators in a modern vehicle but these are the three primary ones that help the vehicle achieve its mission and reach its destination safely.

In the case of the vehicle, the sense–perceive–decide–actuate model describes how a single autonomous system can operate effectively in and with the world around it. A very similar model describes how multiple autonomous systems can also be orchestrated for effective operations. Anduril, a defense technology company founded by Palmer Luckey, the inventor of the Oculus Rift virtual reality headset and founder of Oculus VR, provides a good example of this.

Anduril builds autonomous systems—drones—that operate on land, at sea and in the air. Individually and collectively, they provide decentralized sensing capabilities for surveillance, reconnaissance, inspection, and other intelligence gathering missions.

The company's flagship product, Lattice OS, orchestrates these systems. Lattice is an AI-powered, open operating system that "connects autonomous sensemaking and command and control capabilities with open, modular, and scalable hardware components for a layered family of systems approach. It enables men and women in uniform to move with machine speed, unparalleled confidence, and military-grade security by turning data into information, information into decisions, and decisions into actions across tactical and strategic operations" (Anduril, n.d.).

Lattice includes three of the four functions we described for the autonomous vehicle. They are understand (rather than perceive), decide, act (rather than actuate). Collectively, however, the Lattice OS and the family of autonomous systems cover the entire sense, understand, decide and act model with the drones performing the sense function as well as part of the act function. What it shows us is that the model need not be limited to just one autonomous system but can equally apply to the orchestration of many of them. The four functions can be decoupled from one another and be performed by different parts of the overall system. And because each individual part is connected and autonomous, it has the capability of choreographing its own actions with those of its neighbors or partners, improving their collective responsiveness.

In passing, it's worth noting that Anduril's approach to creating product is not to wait for a contract from a client but rather to anticipate what will be needed and then build quickly and cheaply, applying the same type of flow-based practices that we discussed in Chapter 8 to both hardware and software product development.

How then do these models of autonomous systems apply to Boundless businesses and how might we adapt them to create a Boundless operating model? The short answer is they work very well, but we think the following tweaks are worth making to make them most useful.

First, Boundless companies live as part of markets and ecosystems and communities, not apart from them. The idea of a company going it alone is no longer tenable. Identity is not defined in terms of isolation and exclusion but in terms of connectedness and inclusion. From an operating model perspective, we want to be able to show that a Boundless company is connected to a larger ecosystem and that everything it does happens within the context of that ecosystem.

Second, the models we've shown tend to focus on sensing immediate and/or local conditions, what is sometimes described as situational awareness. This is critical to effective decision-making but nowadays situational awareness by itself is no longer enough. Today's company needs to be horizonally aware as well. Horizontal awareness means being connected to the larger world beyond the immediate here and now. Companies need to be able to see "further down the road" in exactly the same way that an autonomous car can be aware of conditions anywhere along its journey and can take active steps to anticipate and avoid problems, all because of its global as well as local connectedness.

Third, as may have become clear from the discussion of the same model applying to one autonomous system as well as to a "family" of them, Boundless systems are self-similar at various levels (also known as *fractal*). This means that individual resources within a Boundless company are themselves Boundless and have the same responsibility as the company to be responsive to the immediate needs of their customers and to current market conditions, and to be attuned to and prepared for future ones. And just like the company as a whole, when individual employees and teams take action, they do so in the world, not in a vacuum. Our model must place action and reaction in its context, local or global, and it must be able to work at the individual, the team, and the company levels.

The outcome of these considerations is the Boundless operating model (Figure 10.1).

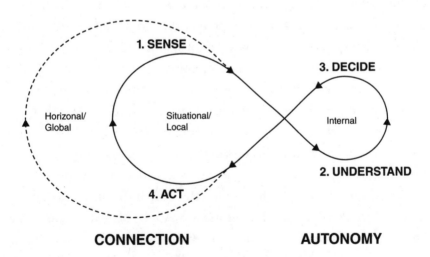

Figure 10.1   The Boundless operating model.

We've separated the four functions discussed into two domains: connection and autonomy. On the left side of the model, the domain of **connection**, we have the sense and act functions that happen in, and in connection with, the larger world of which the system is a part. The point here is that these systems don't act in a vacuum. They act in and on the world and the world acts on them. There are two loops on this side. The smaller loop (solid line) describes the local and immediate world in which the system acts. This is the same as the "situation" in situational awareness. The fighter pilot, the autonomous car, the company, and the team, sales rep, or project team all have to be enabled and equipped to sense and respond to the situation they find themselves in, to react to a car slowing down in front of them, to have the information available to them to respond effectively to a customer call, and so on. The larger loop (dotted line) describes the global and near future or emerging world in which the system also has to act. The autonomous car is not only connected to the other cars around it and knows through its sensors its real-time position relative to them and the other entities on the road, it is also connected to the larger world and knows the emerging conditions further on down the road. As a result it can predict the likely impact on its own "mission" and take pre-emptive actions to avoid it. All companies now have access to predictive and prescriptive data analytics and the successful ones will be those that use them to make informed decisions and take anticipatory action, either to avoid knowable challenges or to seize knowable opportunities or both. We call the dotted loop *horizonal* to express this broader context in both time and space that all companies must be connected to in order to succeed.

On the right side of the model, the domain of **autonomy**, we have the understand and decide functions. Of immediate importance here is that in a post-pandemic, do-anything-from-anywhere world, a company's teams and employees are all increasingly distributed and remote from the center and must therefore be given the autonomy to make timely and accurate decisions about how to fulfill their missions. The company will need to revamp its management and supervision processes in the form of resource orchestration in order to deal with this decentralized and autonomous workforce. We will return to the resource management theme in the context of this model later and will show how and where orchestration itself and other management functions such as planning and forecasting take place. Meanwhile, the company itself must also be autonomous in the sense of having a unique identity and mission, despite its connection and its Boundless nature.

As previously mentioned, the Boundless operating model is designed not only to support the requirement for all companies to have situational and horizonal awareness but also to work at individual and collective levels. Companies can use the model to design and develop processes for individual employees, teams of employees, and organization-wide business management processes.

As a final point, there's broad consensus about the names of each function in the models we've shown, with only a few minor differences. We believe *sense* is more appropriate than *observe* given that this model can apply as well to technology systems such as autonomous vehicles as it can to human organizations. Following Anduril, we prefer *understand* to *perceive* or *orient* because it has more general use. All models agree on *decide*. We prefer *act* to *actuate* again because it has more general use, although we also recognize that this function may involve actuation (putting into action) by the orchestrator component of the overall system and action by the executor component where those components are decoupled from one another. This leaves us with the acronym SUDA (sense, understand, decide, act) for the Boundless operating model.

In short, the Boundless operating model, or SUDA, is an evolution of other situational awareness or sense-and-respond models that are designed to reflect dynamically changing conditions, unlike, for instance, the PDCA or Deming cycle, which was designed for continuous improvement in stable conditions or relatively controlled environments. It places an autonomous entity, be that an employee, a team, or a company, in the context of a connected world locally and globally and it can be used by companies as a conceptual model to identify, define, and develop processes that will enable it to act decisively, learn and improve continuously, and respond at the speed of need in that world.

Relationship Strategy

Business relationships are not a new concept. All companies depend on having successful relationships with their key stakeholders. And yet very few companies actually build their business on them. They tend to be resource driven instead of relationship driven. There are signs that this is changing as companies become increasingly aware of the importance of the experience that their customers have interacting with them, their brands, and their offers. A good number of new roles and skill sets have emerged since the new millennium to focus on the design of those experiences. But experiences do not exist in a vacuum, or at least they shouldn't. Unless there is a goal to build mutually valuable and sustaining relationships between providers and customers, between colleagues, between ecosystem partners, what's the point of focusing on experiences? How do we know what an experience should be like without a context for it? Our view is that organizations need to become more intentional about planning for and then designing for the relationships that they want to have by designing the experiences, transactions, and communications needed to create, nurture, and deepen those relationships.

Where do we start? We can imagine and describe relationships in terms of the type of attributes we would like them to have. And then we can design for them by recognizing them as emerging from the accumulation of individual interactions, by which we mean transactions, experiences, communications, and even our products, services, and brands. This is not an exact science, of course, and the quality of the relationship is not simply an additive accumulation of the qualities of each individual interaction. No doubt we will learn more about relationship strategy and design over the next few years but we know where to start. We need to ask ourselves what does this person mean to us? Why do we want to have a relationship with them? What kind of relationship do we want to have with them? What are its characteristics?

We can start with the basis for any successful relationship, namely, trust. Thanks to work by Rachel Botsman, a leading expert on trust in the modern world, and by other university and corporate researchers, we already know the four main components of trust—and therefore the four things that need to be built into every interaction (Botsman, 2017):

Competence (or capability). The ability to carry out the activities and perform the functions expected of us, individually and collectively

Reliability (or consistency). Doing what we say we will, when we say we will, every time

Integrity (or honesty, transparency). Telling the truth, doing the right thing, without regard for personal consequences

Empathy (or care, benevolence, intent, humanity). Putting the interests and success of the customer first in our decisions and actions

Botsman draws a distinction between the first two of these components and the last two. The first two demonstrate our capacity, what we're capable of doing. The second two demonstrate our character, what kind of a person we are. Losing our customers' trust in our capacity is undoubtedly problematic, but at least it can be resolved through demonstrating our ability to learn and improve and execute. Losing our customers' trust in our character is altogether a different level of problem and is incredibly hard to recover from. So in all interactions we need to be careful to demonstrate these characteristics and never fail from an integrity or empathy perspective.

In addition to trust, what else makes for a successful relationship? Here we are getting into more subjective matters but we believe that the following are ideal characteristics:

Commitment. Showing that we care. Demonstrating that we take the relationship with our customer very seriously and will work hard to nurture it through incrementally additive positive interactions (i.e., bit by bit, one interaction at a time). Interestingly, successful relationships do not seem to be based on the qualities of its individual members but rather on the care that they pay to the relationship itself.

Communication. Keeping our customer informed and up-to-date, especially regarding the status of any transactions between us and any problems or concerns or questions that they have shared with us.

Respect. Demonstrating that we take our customers' lives seriously, we respect whatever it is that they are trying to achieve in their everyday lives as well as in their interactions with us.

Love (delight, magic, enchantment). Creating a relationship beyond the transaction, infusing it with something a little extra, taking emotions seriously. As we discussed in Chapter 3, this may sound fanciful but some companies can and do achieve an emotional connection, as Wegmans and its customers' love letters prove.

Unique identity. Standing out in some way that attracts customers to us and that differentiates us from our competitors.

Mutual value. Being explicit about the value exchange potential, what do we want to get out of our relationship with our customer and what they can expect from us. The members of successful relationships do not need to get the same thing out of it as each other but they do need to feel that they are getting equivalent value.

These characteristics then should be considered when designing the kind of relationship we want to have with our customers. Now, you may want to have different types of relationships with different customer populations or personas. It is not important here how you segment or cluster them, only that you think deeply about the implications for the types of relationships you want to have with them.

Good relationships have always been at the core of successful business. But despite their importance they are rarely prioritized, something to be designed intentionally like products and services and, more recently, experiences. We have made only a few predictions about the future but one of them is surely that we will begin to see relationship strategy, relationship design, and even relationship transformation become core competencies of successful businesses in the not-too-distant future.

Becoming Boundless

Let's get back to where this all started, with the problem of silos. By now we understand what silos are. They are structures in which to accumulate, protect, and control resources in order to extract as much value from them as possible. All the various flavors of "attract and retain" and "do more with less" speak to these principles. And by and large this has worked very well for them when they have been able to generate strong, steady, and predictable demand for their resources. But the world is changing, driven in large part by technological advances, by the increasing power and choice of individuals, and by growing concern for our natural resources and our environments. To maintain relevance our businesses need to change, too, starting with the very principles on which they are founded.

And so we applaud and support everyone who wants to smash their silos, but we understand that when you do so without an alternative you get a spill not a flow. A spill is a waste of resources that can even become a pollutant or a hazard. When we say Boundless we don't mean a spill but a directed, intentional flow of resources in the same way that the blood in our body flows to where it is needed via a circulatory system. Although Boundless is not structure like a silo, it's not nothing. It has its own set of principles and it requires direction and discipline to follow them.

This is an important point that is worth re-emphasizing, especially in light of the more demanding market conditions that have visited us in 2023 as we have been completing this book. Boundless is about shared success but it is not a free for all. There is a risk with the name *Boundless* that it may be misunderstood to stand for unfettered growth and that it signifies a lack of discipline and an insensitivity to issues such as cost and productivity demands. But nothing could be further from the truth. The real question is how are these issues handled in the Boundless model compared to the silo model.

Cost Versus Waste

The most immediate impact of COVID-19 on businesses was that all of a sudden they had to be online to survive. Their customers had to be able to find them and transact with them and their employees had to be able to access their business systems from outside of the office in order to be able to work individually and collectively. All the technology companies and especially the cloud companies did exceptionally well during this period and experienced huge growth at a time when initial expectations or at least fears were that the entire economy would collapse. Things have changed again, however, as the rush to digital has leveled out. Those same companies are now looking to cut costs to counteract their previous growth and to anticipate deteriorating market conditions.

Cost cutting, however, is a silo-based strategy. By that we mean that it is resource management oriented rather than value creation oriented or even relationship building oriented. Even in these market conditions or in business cycles that favor margin growth over revenue or customer growth, we believe that a focus on reducing waste is a better strategy than cutting costs. The reason is twofold. First, all waste has a cost associated with it but not all costs are wasteful. This means that all efforts to reduce or even eliminate waste will cut the right costs, costs that generate no value. At a minimum this means that they will not cut into the "muscle" of the organization and make it less fit. More likely they will actually improve its fitness and responsiveness. In other words, waste reduction is a path to becoming Boundless, one we would recommend in any cycle, and is thus more disciplined and more constructive than pure cost cutting. Second, and related, waste has a negative impact on value to the customer, quality, and/or sustainability. Reducing waste therefore has a positive impact on value, quality, and/or sustainability. This means that reducing waste is always a good strategy regardless of business or market cycle. Third, some waste bears a cost not just for the company but also the world beyond it. This type of waste is known in economics as an externality, a by-product that is borne unwittingly by a third party. Reducing or eliminating externalities has particular relevance in terms of sustainability and helps achieve shared success.

Of course, this makes it sound easier than it really is. It's standard accounting practice to identify, measure, and report on an organization's costs. But not all forms of waste are so easily identifiable or measurable. In particular, business processes outside of the manufacturing industry are rarely scrutinized in any formal way for waste even with the increase in disciplines and certifications like lean six sigma. And business complexity has grown to the point where it can be difficult to trace activities back to customer or stakeholder value. To compound matters further, people naturally favor their own ways of completing tasks and solving problems, even when those ways may be objectively more complicated and more time-consuming than consistent, standardized, or shared approaches. So waste, including nonstandard work, can be difficult to pinpoint and even more difficult to eliminate.

Despite these challenges, standard work is far more effective than nonstandard work. It is easier to automate, cheaper and quicker to onboard, and easier to scale. All efforts should therefore be made to standardize for waste reduction when possible, recognizing that this holds true for process but not for experience, where the goal is to provide customers with personalized experiences based on their specific goals and needs. Nor does it hold true in the same way for disruptive rather than sustaining innovation when the goal is to find new ways of creating value rather than improving existing ways. But even there, standardization can be a powerful source of innovation, not its opposite, and so should not be rejected outright.

Productivity Versus Value

Third, we do care about productivity but not in terms of pure output per input unit but rather in terms of output value per unit, which is to say we care about the desired and actual goal of each unit being the delivery of value to the customer and when relevant to the ecosystem. Productivity without customer demand is just busy work and potentially even wasted or wasteful work.

A suspicion has arisen since the overnight shift from office-based to home-based working in 2020 that employees are less productive than they used to be and that company culture erodes in a predominantly online, decentralized setting (more accurately, a multiplicity of settings). And so we have seen a reflexive swing in the opposite direction based on that suspicion. And yet we remain convinced that over the longer term business will continue to be performed in an increasingly digital, increasingly decentralized way, with working from home or from anywhere being a more time-effective choice for individuals and cost-effective for corporations. Of course productivity is important; after all, employees are paid by the organization to do work, but if we measure productivity in a holistic way based on value then we might ask if the daily commute and the commitment to office space are actually valuable or wasteful. Regardless, technology is going to continue to make virtual work, individual and collaborative, more effective, and, regardless of short-term effects, the longer term is sure to be virtual and hybrid.

In short, leaders should be prepared for virtual work to become the norm. Ensure that everyone in your organization is using the same productivity and the same remote collaboration tool sets, and invest in learning how to work, collaborate, and lead virtually, physically and in hybrid work environments. But go beyond the use of tools. It's easy to delegate learning to technology and it's also easy to default to technology as a scaling mechanism. But you can't delegate identity and culture to technology. Teammates and new joiners in particular may rarely or never meet in person so helping them to onboard, to understand their mission, to connect with others while working virtually becomes an even more important aspect of leadership. The new responsibility of the leader is not to supervise the work of the individual or team but to empower them to perform it autonomously and to operate as "team of teams" as described by General McChrystal in his book of that name. Again as we've seen, autonomy does not mean stand-alone. Rethink how to assert your organization's culture and identity in the absence of a physically identifiable "center." Purpose and values are important contributions here and we anticipate that other shareable traits will emerge over time to help define a company's personality.

One other observation from human behavior during COVID-19, as well as over a period of thousands of years: humans do not need to come together to do work, but they do seem to need to come together for culture, celebration, and leisure. There was no mass quarantine breach by workers who just couldn't wait to get back to the office. And yet it seemed like everywhere there was a swimming pool or a beach a spontaneous gathering and party arose. Thinking ahead we believe that this could well change the design and use of corporate locations and mark the advent of a different kind of company gathering.

Growth Versus Growth

And, of course, we do care about growth, but the Boundless model recognizes that the most sustainable growth is that which is driven by the increase in the numbers of members in the ecosystem and by their well-being as much as it is by the growth of the company itself.

To become truly responsive, organizations across all industries need to rethink their core assumptions about what being successful means and how to achieve it. Boundless is not a tweak or a refinement or a minor change to existing principles and practices. As a result, the answer to "Where and how do we start?" is not found in making operational or tactical recommendations. Leaders and designers need to digest the difference and see how it applies to their own company before such recommendations become relevant.

In Conclusion

Responsiveness to changing needs and conditions, technological, economic, and social, has been the main driver for this book. Even as we have been writing it conditions have changed more than once. Even when we first started writing about silos and about flow in 2014 we believed that business would inevitably move online and become more decentralized, but then of course COVID-19 came along and everything that we had been sensing suddenly became very real. But we knew that these moves would not be viewed by everyone as the beginning of a new way of working but more as an improvisation made necessary by the interruption of an existing one and that we should expect something of a shift back. It looks like we are starting to see that happening as we get ready to finish the book. And yet these forces of change have not abated and these crises are still with us. The need for a new paradigm is as fresh as it was.

Which brings us back to *Boundless* and what it means. As we stated in the Introduction, Boundless organizations are Boundless in the following ways:

- Boundless organizations are Boundless in their energy and their enthusiasm for the success of their customers, their employees, their partners, and their communities.
- Boundless organizations are Boundless in their ability to transcend the physical limits of their office spaces and to become effective orchestrators of their remote, distributed workforce and other resources.
- Boundless organizations are Boundless in terms of looking and acting more like networks than like hierarchies, with different growth and scaling properties. They create close relationships with the other members of their ecosystems, realizing that future growth, health, and resilience is more likely to come

from the ecosystem as a whole than from any one of its individual members.

■ Boundless organizations are Boundless in terms of their situational and horizontal awareness. They're able to sense and respond and to predict and proact.

■ And Boundless organizations are Boundless in terms of their scalability. They've found new ways to manage their resources. And they've learned to manage technology resources—AI, robots, and smart devices of all types—as coworkers with their human counterparts.

This then is the Boundless paradigm. One, it's a new way to think about how companies and institutions should organize and operate, about how customer experiences should feel and about what products should do, and about the world and our place in it. And two, it's a new way to actually do all those things. It's a new model for building business responsiveness and resilience in an ever-changing world, governed by a set of interwoven principles for achieving shared success, realized by resources who are individually empowered to be autonomous, connected, and mobile, and who are collectively organized to be integrated, distributed, and continuous.

Thank you for the gift of your time. We're excited to build a Boundless world together.

Acknowledgments

We would like to thank our editor Kirsten Janene-Nelson for her many improvements to the book, and our team at Wiley: Michelle Hacker, Jeanenne Ray, and Jozette Moses. We would also like to thank our colleagues at Salesforce, in particular Dan Farber, John Taschek, and Kristin Raza, for supporting our efforts.

I (Henry) would like to thank Vala Afshar for being a passionate advocate, champion, and partner in transforming the work into this book; professor Lisa Norton for inviting me to co-teach her class at the School of the Art Institute of Chicago (SAIC) despite her deep dislike for all things siloed; the faculty and students at SAIC and the Institute of Design (ID) for giving me the opportunity to share and develop my early thoughts; Michael Croton for his deep, critical engagement with the work throughout all its various stages; Kelly Costello for introducing me to SAIC and ID and for her thoughtful support and discussion; Brian Solis, Megan Colgan Wiggins, Kevin Farrell, and Annemarie Puma for their important contributions to the themes of relationships and trust; Roger Mader, Terry Moran, Brian Quinn, Stevie Zimmerman, and Chris Zimmerman for their enthusiastic encouragement and support of all my various creative outputs; the crew at Tubac Deli and the management at Four Palms; and Sarah King for, well, everything.

I (Vala) would like to thank Henry King for sharing his incredible wisdom with me, and for being a brilliant partner who was able to capture several years of intense collaboration, spirited discussion, career lessons, and exchange of ideas into our new book. I would also like to recognize my brilliant colleagues at Salesforce for educating and inspiring me every day, including my mentor John Taschek. To our Salesforce customers for generously sharing your collective wisdom to help ignite my innovation philosophy and optimistic view of our collective futures. Ray Wang for being a mentor and collaboration partner for nearly a decade. Our podcast has shaped and validated so many of the guiding principles in Boundless. My parents, James Afshar and Showkat Rafi, are my heroes and the persons most responsible for who I am—thank you for encouraging me to write another book. My children—Donya, Pari, and Vala—are my life's purpose and the most important people in my life. And Stacey, for being my best friend in the world and the person who is most responsible for inspiring me to become a better person.

About the Authors

Henry King is an innovation strategist at Salesforce. He is a former CIO with over 35 years of consulting and executive experience, both in the US and internationally, with expertise in innovation, design thinking, and information technology. He has been published in *Fast Company*, *Huffington Post*, ZDNet, and *Businessweek*. King studied classics at Oxford University and has taught postgraduate innovation and design classes at the School of the Art Institute of Chicago and the Institute of Design.

Vala Afshar is chief digital evangelist at Salesforce. He is a patent-holding inventor, podcaster, columnist, and keynote speaker. With over 1 million social media followers, Afshar is recognized as a top business and innovation influencer. He has written over 500 articles and has interviewed over 2,000 guests on his weekly podcast. Afshar is the coauthor with Brad Martin of *The Pursuit of Social Business Excellence: How to Compete, Win, and Expand Through Collaboration* (2012). Prior to Salesforce, Afshar served as vice president of engineering, chief customer officer, and chief marketing officer.

References

Afshar, V., & Martin, B. (2012). *The pursuit of social business excellence.* Charles Pinot.

Aghina, W. (2020). Enterprise agility: Buzz or business impact? McKinsey & Company. https://www.mckinsey.com/capabilities/people-and-organizational-performance/our-insights/enterprise-agility-buzz-or-business-impact

Anduril. (n.d). Lattice for command & control. https://www.anduril.com/command-and-control/

Atomic education urged by Einstein. (1946, May 25). *New York Times.* https://www.nytimes.com/1946/05/25/archives/atomic-education-urged-by-einstein-scientist-in-plea-for-200000-to.html

Arthur, B. (2009). *The nature of technology: What it is and how it evolves.* Free Press.

Arthur, J. (2015). The Virginia Mason Production System (VMPS). https://www.qimacros.com/pdf/Virginia-Mason-Production-System.pdf

Bansal, C. (2015). Why engaged customers are your best customers: Facts & figures on the value of engagement. https://www.LinkedIn.com/pulse/why-engaged-customers-your-best-facts-figures-value-Chetna-Bansal/

Barber, D. (2010). How I fell in love with a fish. TED Conferences. https://www.ted.com/talks/dan_barber_how_i_fell_in_love_ with_a_fish

Benioff, M., & Langley, M. (2019). *Trailblazer: The power of business as the greatest platform for change*. Currency.

Bialik, K., & Walker, K. (2019). Organic farming is on the rise in the US. Pew Research Center. https://www.pewresearch.org/ fact-tank/2019/01/10/organic-farming-is-on-the-rise-in-the-u-s/

Bieber, C. (2023). Car accident statistics for 2023. *Forbes Advisor*. https://www.forbes.com/advisor/legal/car-accident-statistics/

Botsman, R. (2017). *Who can you trust?: How technology brought us together and why it might drive us apart*. PublicAffairs.

Bouchrika, I. (2022). 101 American school statistics: 2023 data, trends & predictions. Research.com. https://research.com/education/ american-school-statistics

Bova, T. (2020). How Hilton uses the golden rule to drive commercial success. *Forbes*. https://www.forbes.com/sites/salesforce/2020/ 11/05/how-hilton-uses-the-golden-rule-to-drive-commercial- success/?sh=1280f351733c

Boyd, B. (2019). Urbanization and the mass movement of people to cities. Grayline Group. https://graylinegroup.com/urbanization- catalyst-overview/.

Case, S. (2022). *The rise of the rest: How entrepreneurs in surprising places are building the new American dream*. Avid Reader Press/Simon & Schuster.

Centers for Disease Control and Prevention. (2021). Loneliness and social isolation linked to serious health conditions. https://www .cdc.gov/aging/publications/features/lonely-older-adults.html

CIOB. (2023). Megacity. https://www.designingbuildings.co.uk/ wiki/Megacity

Connley, C. (2018). This 23-year-old went from waitressing to earning millions as YouTube's "slime queen." CNBC.com. https://www.cnbc.com/2018/01/30/this-former-waitress-is-earning-millions-as-youtubes-slime-queen.html

Csíkszentmihályi, M. (1990). *Flow: The psychology of optimal experience.* HarperCollins.

Digital.ai. (n.d.). Release orchestration. https://digital.ai/glossary/release-orchestration/

Ellen MacArthur Foundation. (n.d.) What is a circular economy? https://ellenmacarthurfoundation.org/topics/circular-economy-introduction/overview

Fadiman, A. (1997). *The Spirit Catches You and You Fall Down.* Farrar, Straus and Giroux.

Fenn, A. (2023). How to smash a silo. Raconteur. https://www.raconteur.net/leadership/how-to-smash-a-silo/

Field, M. (2020). How Sir Tim Berners-Lee plans to rebuild the internet. *The Telegraph.* https://www.telegraph.co.uk/technology/2020/11/15/sir-tim-berners-lee-plans-rebuild-internet/

Foodindustry.com. (2022). What is a CAFO? https://www.foodindustry.com/articles/what-is-a-cafo/

Fortune. (2023). Fortune 100 best companies to work for. https://fortune.com/ranking/best-companies/

Foster, C. (2019). On the language of the deep blue. *Emergence Magazine.* https://emergencemagazine.org/essay/on-the-language-of-the-deep-blue/

Fotheringham, S. (2018, May/June). The advent of continuous manufacturing. *Pharmaceutical Engineering.* https://ispe.org/pharmaceutical-engineering/may-june-2018/advent-continuous-manufacturing

Friedlander, B. (2022). Tear down academic silos: Take an "undisciplinary" approach. Cornell University. https://news.cornell.edu/stories/2022/06/tear-down-academic-silos-take-undisciplinary-approach

The future of fast fashion. (2005, June 18). *The Economist*. https://www .economist.com/business/2005/06/16/the-future-of-fast-fashion

Gartner. (2022). J. W. CEOs turn a sharp eye to workforce issues and sustainability for 2022–23. https://www.gartner.com/ en/articles/ceos-turn-a-sharp-eye-to-workforce-issues-and-sustainability-in-2022–23

Gindrat, R. (2019). Can autonomous cars make traffic jams a thing of the past? World Economic Forum. https://www.weforum.org/ agenda/2019/12/autonomous-vehicles-mobility-electric/

Goldberg, E. (2022). A two-year, 50 million people experiment in changing how we work. *New York Times*. https://www.nytimes .com/2022/03/10/business/remote-work-office-life.html

Hagel III, J., Seely Brown, J., & Davison, L. (2009). Abandon stocks, embrace flows. *Harvard Business Review*. https://hbr.org/2009/ 01/abandon-stocks-embrace-flows

Hale, C. (2022). Sir Tim Berners-Lee offers grand vision for internet's future. https://tech radar.com/news/sir-tim-burners-lee-offers-grand-vision-for-internet's-future

Hunt-Davis, B., & Beveridge, H. (2011). *Will it make the boat go faster? Olympic-winning strategies for everyday success*. Troubador Publishing.

Illinois.gov. (2005). Open road tolling lanes now available at nine toll plazas on Illinois tollway. https://www.illinois.gov/news/press-release.4543.html

Ingold, T. (2011). *Being alive: Essays on movement, knowledge and description*. Abingdon and Routledge.

Insider Intelligence. (2023). Rise of Mcommerce: Mobile ecommerce shopping stats & trends in 2023. https://www.insiderintelligence .com/insights/mobile-commerce-shopping-trends-stats/

ISS Group. (2021). The negative impact of business process silos on productivity. https://blog.issgroup.com/2021/03/08/the-negative-impact-of-business-process-silos-on-productivity/

Jong, M. (2021). Making the unactionable actionable at Virginia Mason Franciscan Health. GE Healthcare. https://www.gehccommandcenter.com/press-coverage/making-the-unactionable-actionable-at-virginia-mason-franciscan-health

Kahn, S. (2020). Medical data has a silo problem. These models could help fix it. World Economic Forum. https://www.weforum.org/agenda/2020/07/medical-data-has-a-silo-problem-these-models-could-help-fix-it/

Kao, J. (2020). These six intelligences will shape smart leadership in disrupted times. World Economic Forum. https://www.weforum.org/agenda/2020/03/six-essential-intelligences-shape-smart-leadership-in-disrupted-times/

Kelly, K. (1995). *Out of control: The new biology of machines, social systems, and the economic world*. Basic Books.

Kelly, K. (2010). *What technology wants*. Viking.

Kessinger, K. (2017). Smash silos to improve cross functional communication. ASAE. https://www.asaecenter.org/resources/articles/an_plus/2017/november/smash-silos-to-improve-cross-functional-communication

Kimmel, M. (n.d.). Why do restaurants fail. Binwise.com

Kimmerer, R. (2022). The serviceberry: An economy of abundance. *Emergence Magazine*. https://emergencemagazine.org/essay/the-serviceberry/

King, J. (2018). Here's what long checkout lines mean for grocery sales. *Insider Intelligence*. https://www.insiderintelligence.com/articles

KPMG. (2015). An evolution of tolling. KPMG International. https://assets.kpmg.com/content/dam/kpmg/pdf/2015/06/kpmg-toll-benchmarking-study-2015-v2.pdf

Larsson, P. (2023). All-time men's best 4x100m relay. http://www.alltime-athletics.com/m4x100ok.htm

Laskowski, E. (2022). What are the risks of sitting too much? Mayo Clinic. https://www.mayoclinic.org/healthy-lifestyle/adult-health/expert-answers/sitting/faq-20058005

Mandelbaum, R. (2020). What's cooking at World Central Kitchen? A case study in relief. Bloomberg. https://www.bloomberg.com/news/features/2020–12–23/world-central-kitchen-brings-food-and-relief-during-covid-pandemic

Martin, B. (2022). Cooking on the frontlines with Chef José Andrés. *GQ*. https://www.gq.com/story/the-frontline-chef-jose-andres

Martin Roll. (2021, November). The secret of Zara's success: A culture of customer co-creation. https://martinroll.com/resources/articles/strategy/the-secret-of-zaras-success-a-culture-of-customer-co-creation/

McDonald, J. H. (Trans.). (2017). *Tao Te Ching: An Insightful and modern translation*. Qigong Vacations.

McKinsey & Co. (2017, November). A CEO guide for avoiding the ten traps that derail digital transformation. https://www.mckinsey.com/capabilities/mckinsey-digital/our-insights/a-ceo-guide-for-avoiding-the-ten-traps-that-derail-digital-transformations

McKinsey. (2018). Why digital strategies fail. *McKinsey Quarterly*. https://www.mckinsey.com/capabilities/mckinsey-digital/our-insights/why-digital-strategies-fail

McLuhan, M. (1964). *Understanding media: The extensions of man*. McGraw-Hill.

Miller, C., & Rampell, C. (2013, February 26). Yahoo! orders home workers back to the office. *New York Times*. https://www.nytimes.com/2013/02/26/technology/yahoo-orders-home-workers-back-to-the-office.html

Muir, J. (1911). *My first summer in the Sierra*. Houghton Mifflin.

Mulesoft. (n.d.). What is application automation? https://www.mulesoft.com/resources/esb/what-application-orchestration

National Transportation Safety Board. (2005). Multivehicle collision on Interstate 90 Hampshire-Marengo Toll Plaza near Hampshire, Illinois (October 1, 2003). https://Nesbit.gov/investigations/AccidentReports/HAR0603.pdf

NOVA. (2000). Andrew Wiles on solving Fermat. https://www.pbs.org/wgbh/nova/article/andrew-wiles-fermat/

O'Brien, D., Kounkel, S., Main, A., & Stephan, A. (2019). Purpose is everything. How brands that authentically lead with purpose are changing the nature of business today. https://www2.Deloitte.com/us/en/insights/topics/marketing-and-sales-operations/global-marketing-trends/2020/purpose-driven-companies.html

Ohno, T. (1988). *Toyota production system: Beyond large scale production*. Productivity Press.

Ozmen-Ertekin, D. (2011). Traffic jams, delays and mitigation strategies. Hofstra Horizons Research. https://news.hofstra.edu/2011/10/09/traffic-jams-delays-and-mitigation-strategies/

Pattani, A. (2016). 5 success tips from a multimillionaire who went from rags to riches. CNBC. https://cnbc.com/2016/09/16/5-secrets-for-success-from-Zara-billionaire-Amancio-Ortega.html

Pearce, A., Pons, D., & Neitzert, T. (2018). Implementing lean—Outcomes from SME case studies. ScienceDirect. https://sciencedirect.com/science/article/pii/S2214716017300076

Pink, D. (2009). *Drive: The surprising truth about what motivates us*. Riverhead Books.

Popkin, G. (2019). "Wood wide web"—the underground network of microbes that connects trees—mapped for first time. Science.org. https://www.science.org/content/article/wood-wide-web-underground-network-microbes-connects-trees-mapped-first-time

Powers, R. (2020). Kinship, community, and consciousness: An interview with Richard Powers. *Emergence Magazine*. https://emergencemagazine.org/interview/kinship-community-and-consciousness/

Radic, D. (2023). Fascinating grocery shopping statistics to know in 2023. Moneyzine.com. https://moneyzine.com/personal-finance-resources/grocery-shopping-statistics/

Reichheld, F., Darnell, D., & Burns, M. (2021). *Winning on purpose: The unbeatable strategy of loving customers.* Harvard Business Review Press.

Riley, C. (2023). Amazon to close 8 of its Go convenience stores. *Supermarket News.* https://www.supermarketnews.com/retail-financial/amazon-close-8-its-go-convenience-stores

Rohwedder, C., & Johnson, K., (2008). Pace-setting Zara seeks more speed to fight its rising cheap-chic rivals. *Wall Street Journal.* https://www.wsj.com/articles/SB120345929019578183

Root, A. (2022). Tesla may have a path to a $4 trillion market value. Here's why. *Barron's.* https://www.barrons.com/articles/tesla-stock-ev-market-cap-51646425743

Rosenstock, L. (2009). Project-based learning at high tech high. Association for Learning Environments. https://www.youtube.com/watch?v=6rv_rmJYorE

Sankaran, V. (2021). Tesla becomes first car maker to surpass $1 trillion market value. Yahoo! Finance. https://finance.yahoo.com/news/tesla-becomes-first-car-maker-085147904.html

Sawyer, W., & Wagner, P. (2023). Mass incarceration: The whole pie 2023. Prison Policy Initiative. https://www.prisonpolicy.org/reports/pie2023.html

Science for All Americans Online. (1990). Chapter 6: The human organism. http://www.project2061.org/publications/sfaa/online/chap6.htm

Scott, W. (2018). Why data silos are bad for business. *Forbes.* https://www.forbes.com/sites/forbestechcouncil/2018/11/19/why-data-silos-are-bad-for-business/?sh=3a79fb15fafb

Sleeper, N. (2018). New year's projections for last year's hottest non-food products. *The Shelby Report*. https://www.theshelbyreport.com/2018/01/05/2018-non-food-trend-projections/

Solnit, R. (1999). *Wanderlust: A history of walking.* Viking/Allen Lane.

Statista. (2023). Global apparel market: Statistics & facts. https://www.statista.com/topics/5091/apparel-market-worldwide/

Strain, T. (2017). Explaining Elmer's Glue shortage. NBC San Diego. https://www.nbcsandiego.com/news/local/explaining-elmers-glue-shortage/35022/

Suzuki, S. (2011). *Zen mind, beginner's mind*. Shambhala.

Sweet, J., Azagury, J., Ghosh, B., Gruzin, T., Wright, O., & Moore, M. (2023). Total enterprise reinvention. Accenture. https://www.accenture.com/us-en/insights/consulting/total-enterprise-reinvention

Tett, G. (2015). *The silo effect: The peril of expertise and the promise of breaking down barriers*. Simon & Schuster.

Thales Group. (2018). Businesses collect more data than they can handle, reveals Gemalto. https://www.thalesgroup.com/en/markets/digital-identity-and-security/press-release/businesses-collect-more-data-than-they-can-handle-reveals-gemalto

Toffler, A. (1970). *Future shock*. Random House.

Turner, J. (2000). *The extended organism: The physiology of animal-built structures*. Harvard University Press.

Ulrich, R. (1984). View through a window may influence recovery from surgery. *Science*. https://www.science.org/doi/10.1126/science.6143402

US Census Bureau. (2023). Decennial census official publications: 2010. census.gov/programs-surveys/decennial-census/decade/decennial-publications.2010.html

Walton, A. G. (2018). "Forest bathing" really may be good for health, study finds. *Forbes*. https://www.forbes.com/sites/alicegwalton/2018/07/10/forest-bathing-really-may-be-good-for-health-study-finds/?sh=7d0ee7508eb0

Watts, S. (2020). IT orchestration vs automation: What's the difference? BMC. https://www.bmc.com/blogs/it-orchestration-vs-automation-whats-the-difference/

Weiser, M. (1991). The computer for the 21st century. *Scientific American*, reposted by Calmtech. https://calmtech.com/papers/computer-for-the-21st-century.html

Weltering, H. (2020). SpaceX's Crew Dragon has that "new car smell" and flies "totally different" than a NASA Shuttle. https://space.com/what-spacex-crew-dragon-was-like-for-astronauts.html

Wise, J. (2022). How many people own televisions in 2023? (ownership stats). Earthweb. https://earthweb.com/television-ownership/

Wise, J. (2023). Smartphone statistics 2023: How many people have smartphones? Earthweb. https://earthweb.com/smartphone-statistics/

Wohlleben, P. (2016). *The hidden life of trees*. Greystone Books.

Zeng, M. (2018). Alibaba and the future of business. *Harvard Business Review*. https://hbr.org/2018/09/alibaba-and-the-future-of-business

Index